Develop **Four Skills** through **English News**

Japan Association
for Media English Studies (JAMES)
English Education and Media Research SIG
日本メディア英語学会
英語教育・メディア研究分科会　編著

JN088903

L Listening

Input

W Writing

Output

R Reading

S Speaking

4 Skills

SANSHUSHA

本書の音声について

本書の音声は，イギリス人女性とアメリカ人男性，つまり，国籍および性別の異なる英語で収録しました。国際共通語としての英語は，多様な国籍の人々が使っています。音声を通じて，英語の多様性にも慣れていただけたらと思います。

音声ストリーミングサービス（無料）のご案内

https://www.sanshusha.co.jp/onsei/isbn/9784384334951/

本書の音声データは、上記アドレスよりストリーミング再生ができます。ぜひご利用ください。

はじめに

　情報化社会の現代にあって，多種多様なニュースが日々更新されています。大量のニュースの中から，自分に必要な情報を取捨選択する能力は重要です。1つのテーマに関するニュースでも記事によって内容や形式が異なるため，複数の記事を参照することも大切です。参照先を英文ニュースにまで広げることができれば，より有益でしょう。

　英語でニュースを聞いたり読んだりすることは学習者には難しいですが，適切な方法に沿って練習を行えば可能となってきます。また，ニュースによって得られた情報やそれに関する自分の意見を発信することも必要でしょう。本書では，ニュースに関連する事柄について，英語で話したり書いたりする能力も養います。

　「聞く，読む，話す，書く」の4技能という言葉がよく聞かれます。日本人は日本語には4技能を日々活用していますが，英語に関してはなかなか同じようにはいきません。英語を習得する観点からは，まず十分なインプット（聞く，読む）を行い，そのうえでアウトプット（話す，書く）の練習を適度に行うのがよいでしょう。「話す」練習ばかりしていても，他人の話を理解できなければコミュニケーションは成り立ちません。反対にインプットだけをしていても，なかなかアウトプットができるようにはなりません。アウトプットにはアウトプットの練習が必要です。

　このような立場から，**本書のコンセプトは「アウトプットを見据えたインプット」**と言えます。これに沿って本書では，各章のセクションを以下のように作成しました。

章内の各セクションについて

Activate Your Schema

　ニュース記事のテーマに関連した情報や背景知識（schema）を掲載しています。

Active Communication

　テーマに関連した話題について，日常会話ができるよう練習しましょう。

Activate Your Language ①

　メインとなるニュース記事です。読んだり聞いたりしてください。

Develop Your Skills

　ニュース記事を読んだり聞いたりする練習方法につき，具体的に示しています。

・**チャンク**とは，意味のかたまりのことです。英語を読んだり聞いたり，また話したり書いたりする際には，数個の英単語を1つのかたまりとして捉えるようにします。かたまりごとに区切ることを**チャンキング**といいます。英文に慣れないうちは，チャンキングを意識することも大切です。慣れてくれば，チャンクを意識しなくても大丈夫になってきます。

・**シャドーイング**とは一般に，英文を見ずに，英語音声に少し遅れて発話することです。

・**オーバーラッピング**とは一般に，英文を見ながら，英語の音声と同時に発話することです。

Summary Check

ニュース記事の内容に関する質問にこたえる問題です。

Activate Your Language ② Write!

空欄を補う形式の英作文問題です。既出の重要表現を定着させます。

Activate Your Language ③ Speak!

ペアやグループでスピーキングを練習します。〈1〉**Let's talk!** では「比較的身近な話題」を，〈2〉**Pros and Cons**では「賛成・反対の意見を考えられるテーマ」を選んでいます。

Going Deeper

テーマや重要な語彙・表現に関して，より深い知識を掲載しています。

【巻末】Important Sentences　重要センテンス一覧

　1章につき4文ずつ，ニュースや日常会話で役立つ表現を選びました。各章の記事から，インプットやアウトプットで役立つと思われる表現を抜き出して太字にしています。そのまま記事から抜き出したセンテンスばかりではなく，英作文や暗唱に活用できるよう簡略化しました。学習のレベルに応じて使い方を工夫してください。

　たとえば初心者なら，太字部分を中心に覚えたり，日本語文を隠して英文全体を読み意味を考えたり，英文を暗唱したりしてインプット量を増やしてください。英語の知識がある程度あれば，英文を隠して日本語文の太字部分に相当する英語を考えたり，日本語文全体を英語に翻訳したりして，アウトプットの練習に役立てることができるでしょう。

　各セクションで学んだ方法や内容を活用することで，英語学習者の皆様の英語力が向上することを願ってやみません。

日本メディア英語学会　英語教育・メディア研究分科会

代表　桝原 克巳

リーディングのテクニック

「まとまった文章を読む」のに役立つ一般的なテクニックとして，次のことが挙げられます。

> 本文を読む前に，
>
> ・**タイトル**（**headline**）
> ・**小見出し**（**subheads**）
> ・**写真・図表**（**photos / charts**）
>
> を見る。
>
> さらに，<u>第1パラグラフ</u>と<u>最後のパラグラフ</u>を読んで，
> 文章の内容を**予測する**。

　headline や subheads 等を見る理由は，全体の概要がまとまっているからです。また，各パラグラフの1〜2行目には要点が書かれていることが多いので，この点にも気を配りましょう。
　本文を読み進めていく最中も，**文の形式・内容を予測しながら読む**ことは大切です。「予測」するには，知識に基づくことが必要です。文法に関する知識はもちろん，内容の背景知識も重要でしょう。ニュース記事の内容は政治・経済・社会・国際・科学等多岐にわたるため，普段から様々な事柄に注意を向けておくことも大切です。

　なお，ニュース記事の書き方には次のような特徴があります。

① **タイトル**（**headline**）
② **リード**（**lead**：記事の書き出し・第1パラグラフ）
③ **ボディ**（**body**：第2パラグラフ以降）

　最も重要なのは①で，その次が②です。つまり，ニュース記事では**タイトルとリードを読めば，記事の概要がわかります**。それ以上の詳細を知る必要がない場合は，第2パラグラフ以降を読まなくてよいと判断できます。

基本語こそコア・ミーニングで攻略しよう

英文の理解には，動詞が非常に重要です。その中でも特に大事なのが，次の4つの動詞です。

have　　make　　take　　get

これらは極めて多くの場面で色々な使われ方をし，様々な意味を作り出します。1語のみで使われるだけでなく，他の単語とともに熟語や慣用句となることも多くあります。これらの意味を1つ1つ機械的に覚えていくのは効率的ではありません。

このような場合にこそ，コア・ミーニングが役立ちます。コア・ミーニングとは，単語の本質的・核心的意味です。「辞書の最初のほうに記載されている意味」と考えてもよいかもしれません。

(1) have のコア・ミーニング「持っている・所有している」

「持っている」という意味は誰でも知っているでしょう。I have a pen. の意味は「私は（1本の）ペンを持っている」で，誰もが共通の解釈がすぐにできます。それでは次の6つの英文はどうでしょうか。

① I **have** a girlfriend.　（僕には彼女がいる）
② He **has** blue eyes.　（彼は青い目をしている）
③ I **had** a good time yesterday.　（昨日は楽しい時間を過ごした）
④ She **has** a shower every morning.　（彼女は毎朝シャワーを浴びる）
⑤ We **have** lunch together at noon.　（私たちは正午に一緒に食事をする）
⑥ We **have** a lot of rain here in June.　（6月にここではたくさんの雨が降る）

訳に「持っている」がありません。辞書には have の意味として30個以上の意味が出ており，その中に「がいる」「降る」等も含まれています。だからといって30個もの意味をすべて覚える必要はありません。We have lunch together. ＝「私たちは一緒にランチを持っている」というコア・ミーニングから，文脈を考えつつ日本語の意味を考えればよいのです。そして英文に慣れてくれば，いちいち「コア・ミーニング→適切な日本語」を考えることなく，「（昼に）食事をする／ランチをとる ＝ have lunch」と認識できるようになります。コア・ミーニングは，あくまでも英語を理解するための1つの方法です。

なお，「食べる」と言うなら eat lunch でよいのではと思うかもしれません。類似表現が複数あると覚えるのが大変かもしれません。しかし，表現が異なればニュアンスが異なります。日本語でも「食べる」と「食事をする」ではニュアンスが異なります。とすれば，「eat lunch ＝ お昼を食べる，have lunch ＝ 昼食をとる」と日本語のニュアンスの違いにあてはめて考えることもできます。have のほうが食事以外にも幅広く使用されることを考えて，日本語も汎用性の高い「とる」を選択することも可能ではないでしょうか。

(2) take のコア・ミーニング「とる」

He **took** some medicine. の意味は「彼は（いくらかの）薬を飲んだ」です。「薬を飲む ＝ take medicine」を熟語として覚える人も多いでしょう。では，次の英文の意味はどうなるでしょうか。
He **took** some medicine and gave it to her.
「彼は薬を飲んだ」では，後半の「それを彼女に与えた」につながりません。「take medicine ＝ 薬を飲む」と熟語で覚えることもよいですが，同時にコア・ミーニングから「薬をとる」というおおまかな

認識もできるようにするとよいでしょう。そうすれば，この例文で「彼は薬を（手に）とった，そしてそれを彼女に与えた」と捉えることができます。

「電車で行く」は go by train ですが，take the train とすることもあります。have でも書いたように，表現が違えばニュアンスが違います。「take ＝とる」なので「電車をとる」というニュアンス，つまり，交通手段として（車や飛行機ではなく）電車を選び取るということでしょう。また，熟語で take a break は「break（休憩）をとる」ということになります。

（3）get のコア・ミーニング「得る・なる」

日本語で「〜をゲットする」というのと同じようなニュアンスと考えてよいでしょう。

I got well. は「well（元気な状態）をゲットした」，つまり「元気になった」ということです。このように，get は「変化」を表すニュアンスがあります。「病気の状態」が「元気な状態」に変化したということです。「彼女は顔を赤らめた」であれば，今まで赤くなかったのに赤い状態に変化したので，She got red として，どの部分かを示すため in the face を加えれば，She **got** red in the face. という表現ができあがります。

have とのニュアンスの違いを意識しておくことは大切です。I have a cold. ／ I get a cold. の違いがわかりますか。have は「持っている」なので「私は風邪を持っている（ひいている）」で，get は「得る」なので「私は風邪を得る（ひく）」です。後者では「元気だった状態」から「風邪をひいた状態」への変化があります。同じように「風邪をつかまえる（キャッチする）」というニュアンスであれば I catch a cold. となります。実際には get の場合とほぼ同じことを指すのでしょう。

（4）make のコア・ミーニング「作る」

「君を幸せにするよ」という告白の言葉は英語では何というでしょうか。「する ＝ do かな？」と思うかもしれません。答えは I'll **make** you happy. です。「幸せな（状態の）あなた（you happy）」を作る（make）と捉えることも可能でしょう。

ニュース番組で特派員がレポートを終えた後，スタジオのキャスターが特派員に質問をするとき What do you **make** of that? と言うことがあります。コア・ミーニングは「あなたは，それ（that）から何を作りますか」であり，「レポートしてくれた内容からどういうことが考えられますか」というような意味になります。日常会話でも What do you **make** of the new teacher? と聞かれたら「新しい先生についてどう思いますか」といった意味となります。

make は使役動詞としても使われます。I **made** her eat it.（私は彼女にそれを食べさせた）のように，使役動詞の意味は一般に「〜させる」です。では，同じく使役動詞の let を使って，I let her eat it. はどうでしょうか。表現が異なればニュアンスが異なるわけですから，この場合も make とはニュアンスが異なります。make では「強制的に〜させる」で，let では「望みどおり〜させる」です。

このような違いもコア・ミーニングを考えればわかりやすいでしょう。もともと彼女はそれを食べたくないのです。しかし，「それを食べる彼女」を（強制的に）作るのが make です。

ある単語の用法や熟語などの意味を覚えるとき，コア・ミーニングから本質的なニュアンスを感じながら覚えると，英語をインプットするときもアウトプットするときも大いに役立ちます。

CONTENTS

日本郵便がドローン導入

総語数 **185** カバー率：4000 語で **71%** CEFR B2 で **82%**

Activate Your Schema

　近年ニュース等でドローンの話題をよく耳にするようになりました。英語の drone にはもともと「いつも巣にいて働かない雄バチ」や「（ハチ等の）ブンブンいう音」の意味があり，これが無人飛行機 drone の名前の由来との説もあります。ドローンは，第二次世界大戦中アメリカ軍によって軍事用として開発されたのが最初だと言われています。現代では民間利用も急速に増えてきました。使用目的は，農業の効率化，土木工事の測定，危険地帯の撮影等がありますが，物流目的も期待されています。日本郵便は 2018 年，遠隔地等での人手不足を補うため，書類の輸送にドローンを試験的に使用すると発表しました。

Active Communication

　日常会話で役立つ語句や表現に親しみましょう。

A1：やあ，何を読んでいるの？

B1：ドローンのカタログ。1 つ買いたいんだ。

A2：ドローン？　値段がとても高いんでしょ？

B2：いや，全然。1 万円で買えるよ。もっと安いものだってあるよ。

A3：本当に？　そのカタログを見せてよ。わあ，かっこいい！

B3：今すぐ店に見に行かない？

B1：「カタログ」のスペルは，英国等では catalogue。

A2：～でしょ？　aren't they?　[付加疑問文]

B2：全然～ない　not at all
e.g. I'm not hungry at all. まったく腹が減っていない。

B3：～しに行かない？　why don't we ～?　[誘うときの表現]
cf. why don't you ～?　～してはどうですか？　[相手に勧める表現。親しい間柄でのみ用い，目上の人には用いない]

◔)) 01　**EXAMPLE**　　　　　　　　　　　　　　※太字は特に便利な表現です。

A1: *Hi, what are you reading?*

B1: *A catalog of drones. I want to buy one.*

A2: *Drones? They are very expensive, aren't they?*

B2: *No, **not at all**. You can buy one for 10,000 yen. There are even cheaper ones.*

A3: *Really? Let me see the catalog. Wow, they are cool!*

B3: ***Why don't we** go check them out at the shop right now?*

Activate Your Language ①

Read & Listen!

Japan Post to start test deliveries using drones

① Japan Post Co. said Friday that it will start test deliveries using a drone between post offices in Fukushima Prefecture.

JIJI

② The Land, Infrastructure, Transport and Tourism Ministry approved the same day an application by the company for flying a drone without an operator watching the airborne device or an assistant who monitors its movements.

③ In past test flights, operators flew drones with assistants checking the movements of the devices by eye. This time, flights will be conducted without such an assistant for the first time.

④ The mail delivery arm of Japan Post Holdings Co. is expected to start its test flights in early November.

⑤ "It's a big step toward realizing delivery services using cutting-edge technologies," Japan Post Holdings President Masatsugu Nagato told a press conference.

① Co. 会社。company の略
cf. Co., Ltd. 株式会社
prefecture 県

② ministry 省［通例, 語頭は大文字で Ministry］
application for ～ ～の申請
cf. apply for ～ ～を申請する・申し込む
airborne 空輸の, 離陸した, 空気伝達の
③ conduct を指揮する・案内する,（業務等）を行う・処理する 图（道徳上の）行為

④ arm 腕（に似たもの）,（組織等の）部門
cf. ［通例複数形で］兵器・武器
be expected to ～ ～することが予想・期待されている
⑤ cutting-edge 最新鋭の
cf. state-of-the-art も同様の意味
press conference 記者会見

⑥ The test deliveries will be conducted between a post office in the city of Minamisoma and another in the town of Namie, about 9 kilometers apart.

⑦ Packages of documents weighing up to 2 kilograms will be transported to their destinations in about 10 minutes. The postal group aims to put the service into commercial use mainly in remote areas.

[October 27, 2018　JIJI / The Japan News]

⑥ apart　（時間・空間的に）離れて

⑦ weigh　圓 重さがある，に重さがかかる，重要である

他 の重さを量る，に重さをかける，を熟考する

cf. weight 图 重さ・体重，重いもの・おもし

up to ～　～まで

destination　目的地，届け先・宛先

aim　圓 ねらう，目指す（to, at, for）

e.g. aim to be a lawyer　法律家になることを目指す / aim for[at] a new record　新記録を目指す

他 のねらいをつける

e.g. She aimed her gun at me. 彼女は銃のねらいを私につけた（銃を私に向けた）。

put A into B　コア・ミーニングは「A を置く・B の中へ」。

e.g. put the plan into effect 計画を実施する

remote　遠い，人里離れた

Develop Your Skills

〈1〉　最初から最後まで返り読みをしないで通読し，記事の内容を把握しましょう。

〈2〉　英文のチャンキングをしましょう。

〈3〉　チャンクごとに意味をとらえながら読んでみましょう。

〈4〉　チャンクごとにシャドーイングやオーバーラッピングをしましょう。

〈5〉　文章全体を理解するよう，最初から最後まで通して読んだり聞いたりする練習を繰り返しましょう。

Summary Check

ニュースの内容に関する以下の質問に，（　　）を埋めて答えましょう。

〈1〉 When did Japan Post Co. announce that it will start test deliveries using drones?

   − It was (　　　　　) Friday.

〈2〉 When will the test flights with no assistant be conducted?

   − The test flights are expected (　　　　) early (　　　　　　).

〈3〉 Why did the president say "It's a big step" at the press conference?

   − Because (　　　　　　　) technologies will be used in the test flights.

〈4〉 What type of packages will the drones carry?

   − They will carry packages of documents weighing (　　　) (　　　) 2 kilograms.

〈5〉 Where will the postal group provide the drone service?

   − It aims (　　　) provide the service mainly (　　　) (　　　　) areas.

Activate Your Language ② Write!

次の日本語を英語にしましょう。（太字の日本語に相当する英語は，本文で学習したものを使うこと）

〈1〉 私は，D's レストランの接客係のアルバイト**に応募した**。

   I (　　　　) (　　　) a (　　　　　　) job as a server at D's restaurant.

〈2〉 彼女は 2 週間で全快する**見込みだ**。

   She is (　　　　　) (　　　) feel better (　　　) two weeks.

〈3〉 彼は自動車整備士になること**を目指している**。

   He (　　) (　　　　) (　　　) be a car mechanic.

Activate Your Language ③ Speak!

ペアやグループで，以下の課題に取り組みましょう。

〈1〉Let's talk!

身近な話題について，会話を楽しみましょう。

(1) How often and when do you visit a post office?

(2) What effective ways are there to use drones?

(3) What restrictions do you think are necessary to fly drones safely?

〈2〉Pros and Cons

次の質問をし合ったり，Yes や No の根拠を話し合ったりしましょう。

QUESTION：Do you agree that drones should be able to take photos and videos?

－ Yes. The reasons are:

①

②

③

－ No. The reasons are:

①

②

③

Going Deeper

② application は名詞で，動詞は apply です。apply には自動詞と他動詞の用法がありますが，コア・ミーニングは「当てる」です。それぞれの表現が「当てる」からイメージできるとよいでしょう。

【他動詞の用法】

apply a bandage to the wound（傷口に包帯をする）/ **apply** the rule to this case（この事例にはその規則を適用する）/ **apply** the brake（ブレーキをかける）/ **apply** lipstick[eye drops]（口紅をつける［目薬をさす］）

【自動詞の用法】

The rule does not **apply** to this case.（その規則はこの事例に適用されない。）/ **apply** for a position as assistant chef（アシスタント・シェフの職に応募する）

第 2 章 豊洲市場が新たにオープン

総語数 **303**　カバー率：4000 語で **64 %**　CEFR B2 で **74 %**

Activate Your Schema

　観光庁は「世界が訪れたくなる日本」を目指しています。今や，ユネスコが定める日本国内の世界文化遺産は 18 件，世界自然遺産は 4 件に上ります。東京オリンピック・パラリンピックに続いて 2025 年に大阪万博等ビッグイベントが開催される中で，日本の魅力をどのように観光に結びつけていくべきでしょうか。世界有数の規模を誇る東京築地市場は，豊洲に移転されました。近年，この市場が外国人旅行者に人気です。マグロの競り等の物珍しさに加え，市民の台所としての人々の活気と喧騒がその理由でしょう。日常の生活感が観光資源になるというこの事例に，今後の日本の観光発展のヒントが隠されているのかもしれません。

Active Communication

　日常会話で役立つ語句や表現に親しみましょう。

A1：豊洲市場にマグロの競りを見学に行ったよ。

B1：ああ，それをテレビで見たことがあるよ。

A2：競りの場所は築地から真新しい豊洲市場に移ったけど，今なおたくさんの観光客を引きつけていたよ。

B2：最大の魅力は何なの？

A3：その巨大なスケールと活気あふれる雰囲気だと思うな。

B3：外国では一般の人はめったに卸売市場に入れないって，どこかで読んだことがあるよ。

A1：マグロの競り	tuna auction
見学する	observe
B1：テレビで	on TV
A2：真新しい	brand-new
今なお	still
引きつける	attract
B2：魅力	attraction
A3：巨大な	massive
活気あふれる	energetic
B3：一般の人	ordinary people
めったに〜できない	
can rarely 〜	
卸売市場	wholesale market

🔊 03　**EXAMPLE**　　　　　　　※太字は特に便利な表現です。

A1: *Well, I went to observe a tuna auction at the Toyosu market.*

B1: *Oh, I've seen it on TV.*

A2: *The auction site moved to the **brand-new** Toyosu market from Tsukiji, but it still attracted a lot of tourists.*

B2: *What's the biggest **attraction**?*

A3: *Its **massive scale** and **energetic atmosphere**, I guess.*

B3: *I've read somewhere that ordinary people in many other countries **can rarely** enter a wholesale market.*

04

Activate Your Language ①

Read & Listen!

Toyosu market reels in 40,000 visitors on first public day

① A sea of visitors numbering about 40,000 people, including overseas tourists, flooded the Toyosu fish market in Tokyo on Oct. 13 as the facility opened to the public for the first time.

② Long lines formed on a pedestrian walkway that runs to the new market from Shijo-mae Station of Yurikamome Line, operated by Tokyo Waterfront New Transit Corp.

③ In the market, located in Koto Ward, visitors observed sales floors of fish, vegetables and fruits from passages through glass walls and could enjoy sushi and other dishes at about 100 restaurants, many of which were moved from the Tsukiji market in Chuo Ward, which closed after 83 years on Oct. 6.

④ A 28-year-old woman from Hong Kong said that the Toyosu market consists of sophisticated buildings, and the atmosphere differs from that of the smaller and packed Tsukiji market.

⑤ She added with a smile that sushi she ate in a restaurant in the market was extremely fresh.

JIJI

reel in （糸等）をリールで巻く
e.g. reel in a fish 魚をリールでたぐり寄せる

① a sea of ～ たくさんの～
numbering の数に達する
flood （多くの物・人が）殺到する
open to the public 一般公開される

② walkway 連絡通路
run 続く［この意味では進行形は使われない］

③ dish （皿に盛った）料理
［→ p.27 Going Deeper］

④ consist of ～ ～から成り立つ
differ from ～ ～と異なる
packed 詰まった，込み合った

⑥ As for the glass walls that separate the sales floors from visitors, a female visitor, 43, who came with two other family members, said, "Considering sanitary aspects, I'm relieved that sales floors are separated from the route for tourists."

⑦ A small turret transport truck, which is used by workers to haul loads, was also exhibited in the new market. Many people stood in the driver's seat for their family members or friends to take a photo of them.

⑧ The new market opened for business early on Oct. 11 with auctions for restaurants and retailers.

⑨ The public is, in principle, allowed to enter the market from 5 a.m. to 5 p.m. except for Sundays, national holidays and on days when it is closed.

⑩ They can see the tuna auctions, which are popular among tourists, at close hand from a deck exclusively used for that purpose from Jan. 15, 2019.

[October 14, 2018 The Asahi Shimbun]

⑥ as for ～　[通例文頭で] ～に関しては
cf. as to は文中でも用いる
e.g. She said nothing as to the matter.　彼女はその件に関して何も言わなかった。
separate A from B　A を B から分離する
aspect　局面
be relieved that ～　～ して安心する
⑦ turret transport truck　ターレット式構内運搬自動車 (通称:ターレ)
haul　(荷物) を運ぶ
load　積み荷 [可算名詞]

⑨ in principle　原則として
be allowed to ～　～することを認められ (許可され) ている

⑩ at close hand　近くで
deck　(船の) デッキ・甲板, (バス等の) 床・階
exclusively　独占的に, に限って

18

Develop Your Skills

〈1〉 最初から最後まで返り読みをしないで通読し，記事の内容を把握しましょう。

〈2〉 英文のチャンキングをしましょう。

〈3〉 チャンクごとに意味をとらえながら読んでみましょう。

〈4〉 チャンクごとにシャドーイングやオーバーラッピングをしましょう。

〈5〉 文章全体を理解するよう，最初から最後まで通して読んだり聞いたりする練習を繰り返しましょう。

Summary Check

ニュースの内容に関する以下の質問に，（　　　）を埋めて答えましょう。

〈1〉 How many visitors came to the Toyosu market on Oct. 13?

　－ A (　　　　) of visitors numbering about (　　　　　　) people came to the market on the day.

〈2〉 Where did the Toyosu market move from?

　－ It moved from the (　　　　　) market, which had a long (　　　　　　) of 83 years.

〈3〉 Where can visitors observe the sales floors?

　－ They can observe the sales floors from (　　　　　　　　) through (　　　　) walls.

〈4〉 What else could the tourists enjoy in the market?

　－ They could enjoy (　　　　　) fresh sushi and other (　　　　　) at restaurants, and also enjoy standing in a small turret transport truck which was (　　　　　　) there.

〈5〉 When is the public allowed to enter the market?

　－ The public is allowed to enter (　　　　) (　　　　) to 5 p.m. (　　　　　) (　　　　) Sundays, national holidays and on days when it is closed.

Activate Your Language ② **Write!**

次の日本語を英語にしましょう。（太字の日本語に相当する英語は, 本文で学習したものを使うこと）

〈1〉イベントは**一般公開されます**が, 座席は限られていますので予約は必要です。

The events will open (　　　　) (　　　　) (　　　　　　　　), but seating is
(　　　　　　　　　) and reservations are required.

〈2〉その賞品は, 表彰状と 10,000 ドルの奨学金と旅費**から成り立ちます**。

The award (　　　　　　　　　) (　　　　) a certificate, a
(　　　　　　　　　) of $10,000 and travel expenses.

〈3〉行方不明のネコが生きて見つかって**安心した**。

I was (　　　　　　　　) (　　　　) the missing cat was found (　　　　　　).

Activate Your Language ③ **Speak!**

ペアやグループで, 以下の課題に取り組みましょう。

〈1〉Let's talk!
身近な話題について, 会話を楽しみましょう。

(1) Do you want to visit the Toyosu market?

(2) Where do you want to take the tourists who will visit your hometown?

(3) What do you enjoy doing while traveling?

〈2〉Pros and Cons

次の質問をし合ったり，Yes や No の根拠を話し合ったりしましょう。

QUESTION：The Japanese government plans to increase the number of foreign tourists who will visit the countryside or rural areas in Japan. Do you agree with this idea?

– Yes. The reasons are:

①

②

③

– No. The reasons are:

①

②

③

Going Deeper

　記事の headline で使われている reel は，本来「(魚等) をリールでたぐり寄せる」の意味ですが，ここでは比喩的に「人を引き寄せる」の意味を持たせています。さらに第1パラグラフでは，"A sea of visitors flooded the Toyosu fish market" と表現することで，海の大きさや水の勢いによってたくさんの訪問者が押し寄せた雰囲気を表しています。活気あふれる魚市場の話題だからこそ，そのような表現を使用しているところに witticism（機知）を感じます。このようにニュース英語では，読者の興味を喚起する言葉が好んで使用されます。grab（逮捕する←つかむ）や ink（調印する←インク）や grill（取り調べる←焼く）等もコア・ミーニングを想起させ，短い語でインパクトを与えています。ask for「〜を求める」の代わりに (be) hungry for 〜「（空腹で）〜を渇望している」を使用したり，「知らない，気にしない」等の否定的な反応を示すために shrug「（もううんざりだと）肩をすくめること」を使用する等は，五感に訴える表現によって読者の共感を誘う例です。

第 3 章　海外シェフ，日本の料理学校へ

総語数 **319**　カバー率：4000 語で **63%**　CEFR B2 で **69%**

Activate Your Schema

　1970 年代後半，米国で日本食が健康的で理想的な食生活として注目され始め，世界中に広まっていきました。2013 年には「和食」がユネスコ無形文化遺産リストに登録され，2017 年の統計では日本食レストランが世界に 11 万 8,000 店と，日本食は世界の人気料理の地位を確立したようです。こうした流れを受けて，日本料理の作り方を学びたいという外国人も増え，来日する学生が急増しています。ただし，これに伴う問題も発生しているようです。たとえば外国人が作ったものが，本来の日本料理からかけ離れてしまうこともあるといいます。日本料理の質の低下を，どうやって防いでいけばよいでしょうか。

Active Communication

　日常会話で役立つ語句や表現に親しみましょう。

A1：お腹が空いてきたなあ。きみは？

B1：私はお腹ペコペコ。お昼を抜いたの。お昼休みにミーティングがあって。

A2：そうなんだ。じゃ，今から何か食べに行かない？

B2：いいね。何が食べたい？

A3：う～ん，エスニック料理が食べたい気分だな。ベトナム料理はどう？

B3：ぜひ！　実際のところ辛い料理があまり好きじゃないけど，ベトナム料理はすごくいいね。フォーが大好きなの。

A1：お腹が空いてくる
be getting hungry
あなたはどうですか？
How about you?

B1：腹ペコだ。I'm starving.
お昼を抜く　skip lunch

A2：〜しに行かない？［誘うときの表現］　Why don't we 〜？
外食する，食べに行く
eat out

B2：いいね，いいですね［相手の提案などに同意を表す］
sounds good/nice/great

A3：〜したい気分だ
feel like 〜 ing

B3：ぜひ，もちろん［「行かないわけないでしょ？」というニュアンス］
Why not?
実際　actually
をあまり好きではない
not a big fan of 〜
［do not like 〜 very much］
cuisine　料理（法）

🔊 05　**EXAMPLE**　　　　　※太字は特に便利な表現です。

A1：*I'm getting hungry. **How about you?***

B1：*I'm starving! I skipped lunch today. I had a meeting at lunchtime.*

A2：*Oh, really? Then **why don't we** eat out now?*

B2：***Sounds good**. What do you want to eat?*

A3：*Umm.... I feel like having ethnic food. How about Vietnamese food?*

B3：*Why not? Actually, I'm not a big fan of spicy food, but Vietnamese cuisine sounds great. I love "pho".*

Activate Your Language ①

Read & Listen!

🔊 06

Foreign cooks flocking to Japanese culinary schools amid boom in cuisine's global popularity

① With Japanese food enjoying a global boom, culinary training institutes in Japan have seen a surge in foreign students eager to learn how to make the country's traditional cuisine.

② The number of international students has more than doubled, with 424 enrolled in fiscal 2017 compared with 178 in fiscal 2010, according to the Japan Association of Training Colleges for Cooks.

③ Their popularity seems to be a reflection of the 30 percent rise in Japanese restaurants abroad in the past two years, with 118,000 on record as of October 2017. Helping to fuel the boom was the addition of *washoku* — or traditional Japanese cuisine — to UNESCO's Intangible Cultural Heritage list in 2013.

Kyodo News

④ The operator of the Tsuji Culinary Institute and the Tsuji Institute of Patisserie in Osaka said foreign enrollment has more than tripled to 240 in the seven years through fiscal 2017.

---

culinary　料理の，台所の
amid　〜の中・最中に
boom　にわか景気，ブーム

① surge　急増，急上昇
(be) eager to 〜　しきりに〜したがっている

② more than 〜　〜を超える，上回る
double　自 ２倍になる
他 を２倍にする
enroll　登録する，入学する
e.g. 他 enroll her in the club　彼女をそのクラブに入会させる
自 enroll in college　大学に入学する
fiscal 2017　2017（会計）年度
according to　〜によると
association　協会
③ reflection　反映，影響
as of 〜　〜現在，〜時点で
fuel　他 に燃料を供給する，を刺激する，あおる
addition of A to B　AのBへの追加
intangible　無形の
cf. tangible　有形の

④ enrollment　入学者数，登録者数 ［enroll の名詞形］
triple　自 ３倍になる
他 を３倍にする

⑤ "I was stunned by the beauty of washoku's tableware and delicate taste, the spirit of hospitality and everything," said Li Zichen, a 23-year-old from Hangzhou, China, who is studying at the Tsuji Culinary Institute. "There is no border for 'deliciousness.' I would like to become a respected cook, so my hometown folks can enjoy my dishes."

⑥ Most foreign students are from Asia, with trainees from China accounting for 31.6 percent of the total in fiscal 2017, followed by South Koreans (24.3 percent), Vietnamese (15.6 percent) and Taiwanese (14.6 percent).

⑦ Like the students, the Japanese food industry has high hopes the trend will help boost sales of Japanese food around the world.

⑧ Tamaki Bito, head of the planning division at Tsuji Culinary School, said it wants foreign students to learn the Japanese tradition of finding harmony between cooking and nature.

⑨ "We have a responsibility to support the cultural significance of food and agriculture," Bito said.

⑩ In 2016, the government established guidelines setting out the knowledge and skills overseas cooks should possess to produce authentic Japanese cuisine.

[June 14, 2018 Kyodo News / The Japan Times]

⑤ stun 囲 を驚かせる，びっくりさせる
cf. be stunned by 〜 〜に驚かされる
the spirit of hospitality おもてなしの心
respected 尊敬される，評判のいい
folks 人々
cf. fork （食卓用）フォーク
dish （皿に盛った）料理
⑥ trainee 研修生
account for 〜を占める・説明する
followed by 〜 その後に〜が続く

⑦ boost を促進する，増加させる

⑧ planning division 企画課，企画部
harmony between A and B AとBとの調和

⑨ have a responsibility to 〜 〜する責任がある
significance 重要性，意義

⑩ establish guidelines 指針を策定する
set out を提示する，明示する
authentic 本物の，本格的な

Develop Your Skills

〈1〉　最初から最後まで返り読みをしないで通読し，記事の内容を把握しましょう。

〈2〉　英文のチャンキングをしましょう。

〈3〉　チャンクごとに意味をとらえながら読んでみましょう。

〈4〉　チャンクごとにシャドーイングやオーバーラッピングをしましょう。

〈5〉　文章全体を理解するよう，最初から最後まで通して読んだり聞いたりする練習を繰り返しましょう。

Summary Check

　　ニュースの内容に関する以下の質問に，（　　　　）を埋めて答えましょう。

〈1〉　According to the Japan Association of Training Colleges for Cooks, how many students enrolled in culinary training schools in Japan in fiscal 2017?

－ There were (　　　　) students (　　　　　　　　　) in fiscal 2017.

〈2〉　What does the popularity of Japanese cooking schools reflect?

－ It is a (　　　　　　　　) of the 30% rise in (　　　　　　　　) restaurants (　　　　　　　) in the past two years.

〈3〉　What helped to fuel the boom of Japanese culinary training schools?

－ The (　　　　　　　) of *washoku* to UNESCO's (　　　　　　　) Cultural Heritage list in 2013 helped.

〈4〉　How has foreign enrollment changed in two Tsuji institutes in the seven years through fiscal 2017?

－ It has (　　　　) than (　　　　　　　) to 240.

〈5〉　What did the Japanese government do in 2016?

－ It established (　　　　　　　　) setting out the (　　　　　　　) and (　　　　　) overseas cooks should possess to produce (　　　　　　　) Japanese cuisine.

Activate Your Language ②

次の日本語を英語にしましょう。（太字の日本語に相当する英語は, 本文で学習したものを使うこと）

〈１〉 あるコンビニでの恵方巻の売り上げは, **2016 年までの** 10 年間で **2 倍よりも多くなった。**

The sales of *ehomaki* in a convenience store (　　　　　) (　　　　　)
(　　　　　) in the 10 years (　　　　　) (　　　　).

〈２〉 2016 年には, 中国からの観光客がすべての訪日外国人の 24% を **占めた。**

In 2016, tourists from China (　　　　　　　) (　　　　) 24% of all the
inbound tourists.

〈３〉 このラーメン店は, 来**年度**に 2 店舗を新規開店し, **売上**を **増やす** ことを期待している。

This ramen shop hopes to (　　　　　) its (　　　　　) by opening two
new stores in the next (　　　　　) year.

Activate Your Language ③　Speak!

ペアやグループで, 以下の課題に取り組みましょう。

〈１〉 Let's talk!
身近な話題について, 会話を楽しみましょう。

（1）What is your favorite Japanese food? Why?

（2）Which food/restaurant would you recommend to foreign tourists visiting Japan?

（3）If you have a chance to have a homestay abroad, what Japanese food will you
cook for your host family?

〈2〉Pros and Cons

次の質問をし合ったり，Yes や No の根拠を話し合ったりしましょう。

QUESTION：Do you want to eat Japanese food while travelling abroad?

－ Yes. The reasons are:

①

②

③

－ No. The reasons are:

①

②

③

Going Deeper

「料理」や「食べ物」を表す語はいろいろありますが，厳密には，意味合いが少しずつ違います。

❶ cuisine：フランス語の「台所」が語源で「料理，料理法」を意味し，"French cuisine" 等，国や地域，文化に密着した料理を指すときに使われます。一流ホテルやレストラン等で作られ，そこでしか食べられない料理を指すこともあります。(本文①③⑩)

❷ dish：「皿」という意味からもわかるように，「調理され，盛りつけられた個々の料理」を指します。(本文⑤)

❸ food：「食べ物，料理，食品」を意味し，調理せずにそのまま食べられるものにも幅広く使える便利な言葉です。(本文①⑦⑨)

第 **4** 章 ソーラーパワー花壇，自動で水やり

総語数 333　カバー率：4000 語で 61%　CEFR B2 で 74%

Activate Your Schema

　太陽光発電は，再生可能エネルギーを使用する発電の中で普及しているものの 1 つです。最近は一般家庭でも導入可能になっています。東京都葛飾区では，街を花でいっぱいにする活動の一環として「フラワーメリーゴーランド」という花壇を導入しました。この花壇，なんと自動で水やりができるのですが，そのための電源として太陽光発電が使われています。地球環境への負荷が低い太陽光発電への期待は，今後ますます広がっていくことでしょう。

Active Communication

　日常会話で役立つ語句や表現に親しみましょう。

A1：きみの大学には，環境に優しいどんな設備があるの？

B1：私の大学は屋上緑化がされているよ。

A2：すごいね！　他には？

B2：ええと，ソーラーパネルがあるな。きみの大学には？

A3：ソーラーパネルに加えて，雑用水槽があるよ。

B3：これらの設備を通して，環境保護に貢献できると嬉しいね。

◁)) 07　**EXAMPLE**　　　　　　　　※太字は特に便利な表現です。

A1: *What kinds of **environmentally friendly** facilities are there at your university?*

B1: ***A green roof has been installed** in my university.*

A2: *Great! What else?*

B2: *Well, there are solar panels. **What about** your university?*

A3: ***In addition to** solar panels, we have a greywater tank.*

B3: *It's nice that we can contribute to environmental protection with these kinds of equipment.*

A1：環境に優しい
environmentally friendly
cf. eco-friendly　生態系（環境）に優しい
B1：屋上緑化がされている
a green roof has been installed
A2：他には何ですか？
What else?
cf. How else can he act?
他に彼はどのようにできるか？
B2：〜はどうですか？
What about 〜 ?
A3：〜に加えて
in addition to 〜
雑用水槽　a greywater tank
cf. greywater　［灰色のgrey から。米国では主に gray と表記］
中水（上水として生活に使用した水を，下水道に排出する前に再生処理しトイレ用水，散水などに再利用する水）
B3：〜に貢献する　contribute to 〜
設備　equipment［不可算名詞］

08

Activate Your Language ①

 Read & Listen!

Solar-powered Flower Bed Automatically Waters Plants
Panasonic adds mist generator

① The government of Katsushika-ku (Tokyo), Panasonic Corp and Katsushika Full-of-flowers Urban Development Promotion Council concluded an agreement on technical cooperation concerning the "Flower Merry-Go-Round" three-dimensional (3D) flower bed, which automatically waters flowers by using solar electricity, May 30, 2019.

Katsushika-ku

② The Flower Merry-Go-Round is a cylindrical 3D flower bed developed mainly by Katsushika Full-of-flowers Urban Development Promotion Council, which is participated in by local companies, organizations, etc. It is equipped with an automatic sprinkler that powers a pump with solar electricity. It enables to introduce, maintain and manage a flower bed at low costs.

③ For the flower bed, 104 flower pots (13 rows × 8) can be installed, and sunlight can be evenly applied by turning the flower pots by hand (they can be turned by 360°). The height and diameter of the pot are 1,880 and 900mm, respectively.

④ The flower bed has a 12W solar panel on its top and

---

flower bed　花壇
water　に水を与える

① conclude an agreement on ～
～に関しての合意の結論を下す（協定を締結する）
concerning ～　～に関して

② cylindrical　円柱（状・形）の，シリンダー状の
cf. cylinder　円柱・円筒・シリンダー
participate in ～　～に参加する
local　地元の
organization　組織
be equipped with ～　～を備えている・装備している
enable to ～　～するのを可能にする
e.g. The scholarship will enable my son to go to college.
その奨学金は息子が大学に行くのを可能とする。
③ pot　植木鉢，深鍋
evenly　公平に，平等に
diameter　直径
respectively　それぞれ
④ W　watt（ワット）の略語。電力・仕事量の単位

a programmable timer for adjusting watering time in accordance with season and plant. The capacity of the water tank is 200L.

⑤ In April 2017, the three organizations started to install the Flower Merry-Go-Round on the roads and at public facilities and event sites in Katsushika-ku (ward). And, since then, Tokyo Metropolitan Nohsan High School, etc have been engaged in the verification test of the flower bed by examining the amount of watering, the concentration of fertilizer and the growth state of three dimensionally-arranged flowers.

⑥ With the latest agreement, Panasonic's mist generator will be added to the Flower Merry-Go-Round as a cooling measure so that people can stay in public spaces with comfort in summer. The power supply of the mist generator is not the solar panel of the Flower Merry-Go-Round.

⑦ At a regular press conference of the mayor of Katsushika-ku that took place May 30, 2019, a prototype of the Flower Merry-Go-Round equipped with the mist generator was showed. The government of Katsushika-ku aims to install the flower bed at international competition sites such as the sites of the 2020 Tokyo Olympic/Paralympic Games.

[June 11, 2019 Solar Power Plant Business (Nikkei BP)]

in accordance with　～に応じて

⑤ install ～　～を設置する
public facility　公共施設
since then　それ以来
be engaged in ～　～に携わっている・従事している
verification　認証，承認
cf. verify　（正確性）を確かめる
fertilizer　肥料

⑥ the latest　最近の，最新の
measure　対策，処置
comfort　図 快適さ，慰め
動 comfort　を楽にする・慰める
形 comfortable　心地よい，快適な

⑦ take place　起こる，行われる
prototype　原型，プロトタイプ
aim　自 ねらう，目指す（to, at, for）
e.g. She aims to be a teacher.
彼女は先生になることを目指している。

Develop Your Skills

〈1〉 最初から最後まで返り読みをしないで通読し，記事の内容を把握しましょう。

〈2〉 英文のチャンキングをしましょう。

〈3〉 チャンクごとに意味をとらえながら読んでみましょう。

〈4〉 チャンクごとにシャドーイングやオーバーラッピングをしましょう。

〈5〉 文章全体を理解するよう，最初から最後まで通して読んだり聞いたりする練習を繰り返しましょう。

Summary Check

ニュースの内容に関する以下の質問に，（　　　）を埋めて答えましょう。

〈1〉 What is the Flower Merry-Go-Round?

－ It is a cylindrical 3D (　　　　　) (　　　　　　), which automatically (　　　　　) flowers by using solar electricity.

〈2〉 What are the advantages of the Flower Merry-Go-Round?

－ It enables users to (　　　　　　), maintain, and (　　　　　　) a flower bed cheaply.

〈3〉 What is the capacity of the water tank?

－ The capacity of it is (　　　　) (　　　　　　).

〈4〉 What else will be added to the Flower Merry-Go-Round?

－ Panasonic's (　　　　) (　　　　　　　) will be added to it.

〈5〉 Where does the government of Katsushika-ku aim to install the flower bed?

－ It aims to install it at (　　　　　　) (　　　　　　) sites.

Activate Your Language ②

次の日本語を英語にしましょう。（太字の日本語に相当する英語は,本文で学習したものを使うこと）

〈1〉私は長年，このボランティア活動**に携わっている**。

I have been (　　　　　　　　) (　　　　) this volunteer activity for many years.

〈2〉**最新の**ニュースは何ですか？

What is (　　　　) (　　　　　　) news?

〈3〉毎年恒例の会議は来週**行われる**。

The annual meeting (　　　　　) take (　　　　　　) next week.

Activate Your Language ③

ペアやグループで，以下の課題に取り組みましょう。

〈1〉**Let's talk!**
身近な話題について，会話を楽しみましょう。

(1) Do you want to have solar-powered equipment at your place?

(2) What kind of eco-friendly equipment would you like to have?

(3) What advantages and disadvantages of eco-friendly equipment can you think of?

〈2〉Pros and Cons

次の質問をし合ったり，Yes や No の根拠を話し合ったりしましょう。

QUESTION：Will solar-powered flower beds installed in public have good effects on Japanese society?

－ Yes. The reasons are:

①

②

③

－ No. The reasons are:

①

②

③

Going Deeper

　石油に依存しないエネルギーとして注目を集め，エコ電力として知られるソーラーパネル。日本では 1955 年に初めて実用化され，今では一般家庭にも普及しています。

　その他にも環境に優しい装置がたくさん開発されています。以下，環境に優しい装置に関する単語や語句を紹介します。

sustainable design 環境に配慮したデザイン / using recycled materials リサイクル材料の使用 / adding insulation to exterior walls and roofs 外壁と屋根の断熱材の使用 / heat exchanger 熱交換器 / dimmer 光調整器 / LED light bulbs LED 電球 / water-saving 節水の / water-saving fixtures[shower head] 節水器具［節水のシャワーヘッド］

第 5 章 美容外科手術, 日本人の最優先は顔

総語数 **390**　カバー率：4000 語で **61%**　CEFR B2 で **71%**

Activate Your Schema

　2017 年，日本で美容整形に関する実態調査が行われました。米国等と異なり，日本独自の傾向があるようです。手術の対象は，世界では胸やお腹等の全身ですが，日本では顔と頭部が大半のようです。また，美容整形にはメスを使う外科手術のイメージがありますが，日本では少数派で，しわやたるみを抑える注射や脱毛等の「プチ整形」が施術の主流でした。ただ美容医療をめぐっては，気軽に施術を受けた結果，トラブルも後を絶ちません。政府，業界団体，そしてわれわれ消費者が今後考えるべき問題は大きいといえるでしょう。

Active Communication

　日常会話で役立つ語句や表現に親しみましょう。

A1：美容整形するのって考えたことある？

B1：まさか！　ぞっとするよ，そうじゃない？

A2：かもねぇ。二重瞼にした友達がいるんだけど，最近ちょっと問題が出てきてるみたい。

B2：どうしたの？

A3：目が少しはれてきたらしいんだ。

B3：大変だね。美容整形手術を受ける前に，リスクをよく理解する必要があるね。

A1：～を考える，検討する
think about
美容整形する
get plastic surgery

B1：ぞっとする，怖い，おっかない　scary
そうじゃない？ ～でしょ？
doesn't it?　[付加疑問文]

A2：二重瞼にする
give eyelids a fold

A3：～らしい，～と聞いた
I heard that ～

B3：(それは) 大変だね，残念ですね　That's too bad.
手術を受ける　undergo
[have] surgery/an operation

◁)) 09　**EXAMPLE**　　　　　※太字は特に便利な表現です。

A1: *Have you ever thought about getting plastic surgery?*

B1: *No way! It sounds so scary, doesn't it?*

A2: *Maybe. I have a friend who had her eyelids given a fold. She had a problem with her eyes.*

B2: *What happened?*

A3: *I heard her eyes have been swollen a bit.*

B3: *That's too bad. You need to understand the risks well before undergoing plastic surgery.*

Activate Your Language① Read & Listen!

Facial looks top priority for Japanese in cosmetic surgery

① Japanese, it seems, are more conscious about their facial looks than their counterparts overseas, according to a study of cosmetic surgeries performed in this country last year.

Imaginechina /JIJI PRESS PHOTO

② The survey by the Japan Society of Aesthetic Plastic Surgery found that about 90 percent of cosmetic surgeries involved facial treatment, whereas the norm overseas is around 40 percent.

③ The remainder involved body contouring, such as breast enhancement and liposuction.

④ "The percentage was higher than we had expected," said Kotaro Yoshimura, a professor of plastic and reconstructive surgery at Jichi Medical University who headed the research project undertaken by the society. "The result suggested there is still a strong aversion in Japan to full-fledged surgery."

⑤ It noted that 1,903,898 medical cosmetic treatments were carried out in Japan in 2017. Of these, about 15 percent involved surgery, while the rest were nonsurgical procedures.

---

cosmetic surgery　美容外科

① be conscious about 〜　〜について意識している・気にしている
counterpart　（対の）片方
according to　〜によると

② aesthetic plastic surgery　美容外科手術
treatment　治療（法）
whereas 〜　〜であるのに，〜に反して
norm　標準

③ contour　輪郭，外形
liposuction　脂肪吸引法，リポサクション

④ still　今なお
aversion　嫌悪（感）
full-fledged　（鳥が）羽毛の生えそろった，一人前の，資格が十分な

⑤ carry out　実行する，実施する
the rest　残り

⑥ The JSAPS said the figure reflected 80 percent of cosmetic surgeries performed last year as it received replies from many large hospitals. It estimated that 60 percent of nonsurgical procedures given last year were included.

⑦ The most frequently performed cosmetic surgery was giving eyelids a fold, accounting for half of all the operations.

⑧ This was followed by facial thread lift to remove saggy skin, nose job, fixing drooping eyelids, removing wrinkles around the eyes and augmentation rhinoplasty.

⑨ Overall, more than 90 percent of the cosmetic surgeries were facial.

⑩ Body contouring such as breast enhancement and liposuction for the torso and limbs represented 3-5 percent of plastic surgeries.

⑪ Of cosmetic surgeries overseas, 40 percent were performed on the face, 30 percent on breasts, and the same percentage on the torso and limbs, according to the JSAPS.

⑫ The survey, the first of its kind in Japan, was conducted in response to calls for a fuller picture of the Japanese aesthetic medical market after it was pointed out that many segments of the industry remain murky.

⑬ The JSAPS, in collaboration with the Japan Society of Aesthetic Surgery and the Society of Aesthetic Dermatology, sent questionnaires to 3,656 medical institutions. It received responses from 521 institutions, or 14 percent.

⑭ Problems associated with medical cosmetic treatments are commonly reported in Japan.

⑥ figure　数字，合計，総額
estimate　見積もる，推定する

⑦ account for ～　～を占める・説明する

⑧ followed by ～　その後に～が続く
saggy　たるんだ，たれ下がった
droop　うなだれる，たれる，弱る
augmentation　増加，増大
rhinoplasty　鼻形成（術）
augmentation rhinoplasty　隆鼻術

⑩ torso　（人体の）胴
limb　（人・動物の）手足（の１本），（胴体・頭部と区別して）肢

⑫ conduct　を指揮する・案内する，（業務等）を行う・処理する
図（道徳上の）行為
in response to　～に応じて
remain　のままである
murky　暗くて陰気な，やましい，不透明な
⑬ dermatology　皮膚病学，皮膚科
questionnaires　アンケート

⑮ The government-affiliated National Consumer Affairs Center's figures showed that cases of grievance reported to the center averaged 2,000 annually.

⑯ Yoshimura said the JSAPS will work to ensure more transparency in plastic surgeries, including costs.

[July 25, 2018 The Asahi Shimbun]

⑮ National Consumer Affairs Center 国民生活センター
grievance 不平, 不満

Develop Your Skills

〈1〉 最初から最後まで返り読みをしないで通読し，記事の内容を把握しましょう。

〈2〉 英文のチャンキングをしましょう。

〈3〉 チャンクごとに意味をとらえながら読んでみましょう。

〈4〉 チャンクごとにシャドーイングやオーバーラッピングをしましょう。

〈5〉 文章全体を理解するよう，最初から最後まで通して読んだり聞いたりする練習を繰り返しましょう。

Going Deeper

⑯ 語頭に en- が付いた単語ですぐに思い浮かぶのは，enjoy かもしれません。この語は en + joy の2つの要素からできています。en は接頭辞（prefix）といい，新語が生まれる過程で加えられる，ある意味を成す文字または文字群の1つです。中でも en は，後に続く形容詞もしくは名詞を，「その状態にする」という機能を持ちます。本文中の ensure は，en + sure（＝確か）という形容詞が合体し，「確実にする」という動詞となります。
　たとえば，以下の要素 -able, -circle, -light, -rich, -title, -vision にそれぞれ en- を付けると，動詞としてどんな意味や働きを持つでしょうか？　考えてみてください。

ニュースの内容に関する以下の質問に，（　　　）を埋めて答えましょう。

〈1〉 What are Japanese people more conscious about than their counterparts overseas?

　　－ They are more conscious about their (　　　　　　) (　　　　　　).

〈2〉 What did most of cosmetic surgeries involve in Japan?

　　－ They involved (　　　　　) (　　　　　　　　).

〈3〉 What did the research project undertaken by the society in 2017 suggest?

　　－ The result suggested that there is still a strong (　　　　　　　　) in Japan to (　　　　　　　) surgery.

〈4〉 What was the most frequently performed cosmetic surgery in Japan?

　　－ It was giving (　　　　　　) a (　　　　　　), accounting for half of all the (　　　　　　).

〈5〉 What will the JSAPS work to ensure?

　　－ It will work to ensure more (　　　　　　　　) in plastic surgeries, including (　　　　　　).

次の日本語を英語にしましょう。（太字の日本語に相当する英語は，本文で学習したものを使うこと）

〈1〉 女性の中には体重をひどく気にする人がいるが，**それに対して**，それほど多くの男性は女性の体重をあまり考えていない。

　　Some (　　　　　　) are terribly self-conscious about their weight,
　　(　　　　　　) few men give it much thought.

〈2〉 私は**予想していたよりも**その試験がはるかに簡単に感じた。そのためにしっかり準備していたからだ。

　　I felt the examination was much easier (　　　　　) I (　　　　　)
　　(　　　　　　　　), because I had prepared hard for it.

〈3〉新入社員研修の間に，詳細なアンケートが**実施される**だろう。

A detailed survey will be (　　　　　　　　) (　　　　　　　) during the new employee workshop.

Activate Your Language③

ペアやグループで，以下の課題に取り組みましょう。

〈1〉Let's talk!
身近な話題について，会話を楽しみましょう。

(1) What parts of your face do you like and dislike?

(2) How much time do you spend getting ready in the morning?

(3) How much do you think people pay for a popular plastic surgery procedure?

〈2〉Pros and Cons
次の質問をし合ったり，Yes や No の根拠を話し合ったりしましょう。

QUESTION：Suppose you have a friend who wants to have plastic surgery. Do you support his/her decision?

－ Yes. The reasons are:

①

②

③

－ No. The reasons are:

①

②

③

第 6 章　仏教寺院でイスラム教を学ぶ

総語数 **402**　カバー率：4000 語で **67 %**　CEFR B2 で **75 %**

Activate Your Schema

　イスラム教徒（約 16 億人）の数はキリスト教徒（約 21 億人）に次いで多いです。日本を訪れるイスラム教徒（Muslim）も増えています。イスラム教の戒律は礼拝やラマダン（断食月）や食事の制限等があり，日本での生活が不便なこともあります。その上，一部では過激な思想と思われることもあるようです。国際社会では，他者の文化や宗教を理解することは重要です。大分県のある僧侶は，イスラム教を理解するための活動を行っています。彼は何を考え，どのような活動を行っているのでしょうか。

Active Communication

　日常会話で役立つ語句や表現に親しみましょう。

A1：今日，デパートで「祈祷室」と書かれている表示を見て驚いたよ。

B1：イスラム教徒たちがお祈りをするための部屋だね。

A2：そうだよね。彼らにはとても役立つだろうね。

B2：知ってのとおり，観光客は言うまでもなくビジネスパーソンや学生がますます多く来日しているからね。

A3：うん。異文化についてもっと学ぶべき時だね。

B3：異なる価値観に敬意を示すことが大切だと思うよ。

A1：表示　sign
　　〜と書かれている
　　saying 〜
e.g. the sign saying "No Smoking"
　　「禁煙」と書かれている掲示
　　祈り，祈祷　prayer
B1：イスラム教徒　Muslim
A2：〜に役に立つ
　　helpful for [to] 〜
B2：〜は言うまでもなく
　　not to mention 〜
　　[without mentioning 〜]
A3：〜すべき時　it's time to 〜
　　〜について学ぶ　learn about
B3：価値観　values

🔊 11　**EXAMPLE**　　　　　　　　　　※太字は特に便利な表現です。

A1: *Well, I was surprised to see a sign **saying** "Prayer Room" in a department store today.*

B1: *That's the space for Muslims to pray in.*

A2: *Yes. It may be very helpful for them.*

B2: *As you know, more and more business people and students are coming to Japan, **not to mention** tourists.*

A3: *Yes. I guess **it's time to** learn more about different cultures.*

B3: *I really think showing respect to different values is important.*

12 # Activate Your Language ①

Oita Prefecture temple holding study meetings on Islam to spread understanding

① A Buddhist temple in Oita Prefecture is hosting a series of learning opportunities on Islam to give people a chance to learn about one of the world's most practiced religions.

② Amid an increase in the number of Muslims studying in Japan or visiting as tourists, exchange activities are expanding.

③ During an April meeting, attendees heard speeches from Daido Jikaku, deputy chief priest of Zenryuji, a Zen temple in Nakatsu, and Altaf Khan, imam of Beppu Masjid, a mosque in Beppu. Longtime Japan resident and practicing Muslim Sayeed Zafar also spoke during the meeting. Attendees learned about Islamic teachings and customs and asked questions about the faith, such as whether it is acceptable to invite Muslims to hot springs.

④ Jikaku, 43, organizes exchange activities with Beppu Masjid, which became the first mosque in Kyushu when it was established nine years ago, and delivers speeches on Islam at local festivals. He started such activities after an Afghan Muslim colleague, who worked alongside Jikaku at an international nongovernmental organization for educational support, apologized for the destruction of the famed Buddha statues of Bamiyan by the Taliban, an Islamist extremist group.

⑤ Realizing that he did not know much about Islam despite the fact that Muslims had protected the Buddhist statues for more than 1,000 years, Jikaku decided to learn more about the religion. After returning to the temple four years ago, Jikaku felt anxious that people around him might believe that Islam is tantamount to terrorism.

---

prefecture　県

① Buddhist　仏教徒
cf. Buddhism　仏教
host　（会）を主催する
learn about 〜　〜について学ぶ
practice　（宗教の教え等）を実践する
② amid　〜の中・最中に

③ attendee　出席者
（接尾語 –ee は「人」を表す。
e.g. absentee 欠席者, refugee 難民）
deputy chief priest　副住職
imam　イスラム教の導師
Masjid　イスラム教の礼拝堂
resident　居住者
hot spring　温泉
④ deliver a speech　講演（演説）をする
colleague　同僚
nongovernmental organization　非政府組織（NGO）
apologize for 〜　〜に対して謝罪する [I am sorry. より改まった表現]
the Buddha statues of Bamiyan　紀元5〜6世紀に彫られたアフガニスタンのバーミヤン渓谷の巨大な磨崖仏
（2001年にタリバンによって破壊された。東西文明の中継地バーミヤンの遺跡群はシルクロードの中でも文化的意義が大きく，各国の支援の下，修復活動が始まっている）
Islamist extremist group　イスラム過激派（グループ）
⑤ despite the fact that 〜　〜という事実にもかかわらず
feel anxious that 〜　〜を不安に思う
be tantamount to 〜　〜にも等しい（to に続く語は否定的な意味を持つ場合が多い）

Courtesy of Daido Jikaku

⑥ "I'll continue grass-roots efforts so people do not consider ordinary Muslims to be the same as extremists," Jikaku said.

⑦ Sayeed, who came to Japan from Pakistan 18 years ago as a student, runs a used vehicle sales business in Beppu.

⑧ He feels that living here now is easier than when he arrived, thanks to an increasing number of places for prayer and supermarkets offering halal foods.

⑨ Muslims are often "isolated" in communities, Sayeed said, and People may feel fear when they see Muslims with beards and wearing turbans, but the meetings can lead to "mutual understanding."

⑩ The meeting in April was joined by some 20 local residents, including Buddhist supporters of the temple.

⑪ The participants talked to the speakers after the study session, viewing the meeting with Muslims as a rare opportunity.

⑫ "I feel that Muslims and Japanese people may be similar in their sincerity and ways of living," a 68-year-old business owner in Nakatsu, said.

[May 25, 2018 JIJI / The Japan Times]

⑥ grass-roots efforts　草の根運動
cf. the grass roots　一般大衆
consider A to be B　AをBであ
ると考える

⑦ run　を経営する

⑧ an increasing number of ～
～が増えている（コア・ミーニン
グは「～の増加中の数字」）
prayer　祈り，祈祷
offer　を提供する
halal foods　ハラール食
（イスラム教の細かな戒律にのっとり
処理，調理された食品）
⑨ beard　あごひげ
cf. mustache　口ひげ
　　whiskers　ほおひげ
lead to ～　～（という結果）につ
ながる
⑩ local　地元の

⑪ study session　勉強会
view A as B　AをBと見る，み
なす

⑫ be similar in ～　～の点で類似
している

Develop Your Skills

〈1〉 最初から最後まで返り読みをしないで通読し，記事の内容を把握しましょう。

〈2〉 英文のチャンキングをしましょう。

〈3〉 チャンクごとに意味をとらえながら読んでみましょう。

〈4〉 チャンクごとにシャドーイングやオーバーラッピングをしましょう。

〈5〉 文章全体を理解するよう，最初から最後まで通して読んだり聞いたりする練習を繰り返しましょう。

Summary Check

ニュースの内容に関する以下の質問に，（　　　）を埋めて答えましょう。

〈1〉 Why has a Buddhist temple in Oita Prefecture been hosting study meetings?

－ To (　　　　　　　) people a chance to (　　　　　　　) about Islam.

〈2〉 What did the attendees hear at the April meeting?

－ They (　　　　　　) two speeches that Daido Jikaku and Altaf Khan
(　　　　　　　).

〈3〉 For what purpose will the priest of the Zen temple continue grass-roots efforts?

－ So that people do not (　　　　　　　) ordinary Muslims (　　　)
(　　　) the same as extremists.

〈4〉 Why does the man from Pakistan now feel it is easier to live in Japan than when he arrived?

－ Because the number of places for (　　　　　　　) and supermarkets
offering halal foods (　　　) (　　　　　　　).

〈5〉 According to the man from Pakistan, what kind of change will the meetings bring people?

  – Although people may feel (   ) when they see Muslims with beards and wearing turbans, the meetings will bring them (   ) (   ).

Activate Your Language ② — Write!

次の日本語を英語にしましょう。（太字の日本語に相当する英語は, 本文で学習したものを使うこと）

〈1〉 全国的な議論**のさなか**, 独立についての国民投票が行われた。

(   ) a nationwide debate, the referendum on (   ) was held.

〈2〉 その会社の CEO は世界経済の不安が増加している**という事実にもかかわらず**, 従来の方針を変えなかった。

The CEO of the company didn't change the conventional policy (   ) (   ) (   ) (   ) uncertainty in the world economy was increasing.

〈3〉 人々はその新技術を成功への鍵だと**みなした**。

People (   ) the new technology (   ) a key to success.

Activate Your Language ③ — Speak!

ペアやグループで, 以下の課題に取り組みましょう。

〈1〉Let's talk!
身近な話題について, 会話を楽しみましょう。

(1) What are the most widely practiced religions in the world? Name four of them.

(2) Which country has the largest number of Muslims in the world?

(3) What would you like to ask if an exchange student comes to your class?

〈2〉Pros and Cons

次の質問をし合ったり，Yes や No の根拠を話し合ったりしましょう。

QUESTION：Imagine the following case and answer the question.

"Your college is planning to begin a service of halal foods in the school cafeteria for the students who need them. The service will cost extra money. In order to cover the extra cost, the price of every dish in the cafeteria where all the students eat will be raised by 100 yen."

Do you agree with this plan to introduce halal foods into your school cafeteria?

－ Yes. The reasons are:

①

②

③

－ No. The reasons are:

①

②

③

Going Deeper

① practice と聞いてまず思い起こすのは，❶「（楽器，運動等を）繰り返し練習する」の意味でしょう。この他，❷「（医師・弁護士が）開業する，営業する」意味にも使われ，medical practitioner と名詞になれば「開業医」を指します。また，❸「（宗教を）実践する，行う」という意味もあります。practice の3つの語義は別々なものにも見えますが，コア・ミーニングは「ある動作／役割／宗教儀式を，定期的に／反復的に実践すること」です。語源はギリシャ語で「行うこと」を意味します。このようにコア・ミーニングを考え適宜語源を参照することは，語彙を習得する上でとても有効です。ことわざの "Practice makes perfect." のとおり，英語学習も「継続は力なり」です。

第 7 章 プラスチックを食べる バクテリアの研究競争

総語数 **406**　カバー率：4000 語で **67 %**　CEFR B2 で **69 %**

Activate Your Schema

　プラスチックごみは環境汚染，とりわけ海洋汚染を引き起こし，世界規模の重大問題となっています。その原因の 1 つは，プラスチックが生物分解できないことです。ところが 2016 年に，世界中の研究者を驚かせる出来事が起きました。プラスチックの原料ポリエチレンテレフタレート（PET）を分解するバクテリアが，大阪府堺市のリサイクル施設のごみの山から発見されたのです。それは「イデオネラ・サカイエンシス」と名づけられました。現在，各国でこのバクテリアに関する研究競争が起きています。もしごみ処理に実用化されるならば，ごみ問題の大きな解決策になるかもしれません。

Active Communication

　日常会話で役立つ語句や表現に親しみましょう。

A1：ペットボトルを食べるバクテリアが発見されたのを知ってる？

B1：いや，聞いたことがないよ。すごい発見だね。

A2：そのとおり！　プラスチックごみを減らすのに役立つかもしれないね。

B2：科学者はいつごろそれが実用化すると言っているの？

A3：時間がかかるだろうと言っているよ。

B3：彼らが早く成功するといいね。

🔊 13　**EXAMPLE**　　　　　　　　　　　※太字は特に便利な表現です。

A1: *Did you know a kind of bacteria that eats plastic bottles has been discovered?*

B1: *No, **I haven't heard about that**. It's a great finding.*

A2: *Yes! It could help to reduce plastic waste.*

B2: ***When do scientists say it will put it into practical use?***

A3: *They say **it will take a long time**.*

B3: *I hope they will make it soon.*

A1：ペットボトル
plastic bottle
バクテリア，細菌
bacterium　ただし，通例
圈 bacteria が用いられる。

B1：それについて聞いたことがない。
I haven't heard about that.
cf. I've never heard of that. は通例その言葉の意味を知らない場合に用いる。

A2：減らす　reduce

B2：疑問詞 + do you say [think/suppose/believe/imagine] ～？
e.g. Where do you think he lives? あなたは彼がどこに住んでいると思いますか？

A3：（長い）時間がかかる
it takes a long time
cf. It takes 10 minutes to walk to the station.　駅に歩いて行くのに 10 分かかる。

B3：成功する，うまくやり遂げる　make it

Activate Your Language ①　Read & Listen!

14

Tiny organism that eats plastic spawns race to tap its secrets

① A bacterium that gorges on PET bottles has spurred a global research race to harness its powers in the battle against plastics pollution in the world's oceans.

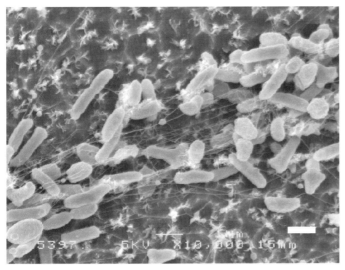

Shosuke Yoshida of the Nara Institute of Science and Technology

② The bacterium was given the name Ideonella sakaiensis in 2005, as it was found in soil samples at a plastic bottle processing plant in Sakai, Osaka Prefecture.

③ Methods for dealing with the contamination of marine environments by plastics is expected to be a major theme of the Group of 20 summit to be held in Osaka on June 28-29.

④ Kohei Oda, now professor emeritus of applied biology at the Kyoto Institute of Technology, was among those who were part of a team that discovered the bacterium.

⑤ Subsequent research by Shosuke Yoshida, now a specially appointed associate professor of environmental microbiology at the Nara Institute of Science

---

spawn　（魚・蛙等が）（卵）を産む，〜を大量に引き起こす

① gorge on 〜　〜をガツガツ食べる
PET = polyethylene telephthalate ポリエチレン・テレフタレート
spur 〜　〜に拍車をかける
harness 〜　〜を利用する

② Ideonella sakaiensis　イデオネラ・サカイエンシス（ペットボトルの原料を分解して栄養源にしている細菌の名前）
processing plant　加工工場，処理工場
prefecture　県（ここでは「府」）
③ deal with 〜　〜に対処する，〜を処理する
contamination　汚染
be expected to 〜　〜することが予想・期待されている
theme　テーマ
④ professor emeritus　名誉教授
applied biology　応用生物学
those who 〜　〜する人々

⑤ subsequent　次の，後続の

and Technology, found that the bacterium used two enzymes to decompose polyethylene terephthalate (PET), a synthetic resin widely used in plastic products.

⑥ The bacterium was found to consume PET film with a thickness of 0.2 millimeter in about a month while decomposing it into carbon dioxide and water.

⑦ PET was long believed not to be biodegradable, as it is produced using petroleum.

⑧ But when Oda and others released an article in an academic journal in 2016 about how Ideonella sakaiensis feeds on plastic bottles, the global scientific community was stunned.

⑨ Inquiries came in from fiber and other manufacturing companies around the world, and a race to uncover how the enzymes break down PET was also triggered.

⑩ In 2017, a team of Chinese scientists released its finding of the analysis of the structure of one of the enyzmes, dubbed PETase, and published it in a British journal.

⑪ That was followed by other articles by South Korean and Chilean teams that provided greater detail into the enzyme structure.

⑫ A British team succeeded in improving the ability of the enzyme to decompose plastic, leading the BBC to report that the finding could set off a revolution in PET bottle recycling and more effective reuse of plastics.

⑬ This year, a German team succeeded in creating a 3-D analysis of the other enzyme, MHETase.

⑭ Yoshida and other scientists have joined the international effort to determine what conditions allow the enzymes to break down plastics in a more efficient

enzyme 酵素
decompose ～ ～を分解する
synthetic resin 合成樹脂

⑥ consume ～ ～を消費する
carbon dioxide 二酸化炭素

⑦ biodegradable 生(物)分解可能な
petroleum 石油

⑧ article 論文，記事
academic journal 学術誌
feed on ～ ～を常食とする
stun を驚かせる，びっくりさせる

⑨ inquiry 問合せ
uncover ～ ～を明らかにする
trigger 他(銃の)引き金を引く，(事件等)を引き起こす

⑩ dub A B A に B（あだ名）をつける
PETase ペターゼ（Ideonella sakaiensis から 2016 年に発見された酵素）

⑪ followed by ～ その後に～が続く
Chilean チリ（人）の
cf. Chile チリ
detail 詳細
⑫ set off ～ ～を引き起こす
revolution 大改革，革命

⑬ MHETase 酵素の名前（PETase とともに Ideonella sakaiensis に含まれ PET を分解する酵素）

⑭ allow A to do Aが（～するのを）許可する，可能にする
manner 方法，やり方

manner.

⑮ "Although I believe it will take time, I am hopeful that the bacterium found in Sakai will become the catalyst for a resolution of the plastic problem," Oda said.

[June 21, 2019 The Asahi Shimbun]

⑮ catalyst　触媒（の働きをする人［もの］），きっかけ
resolution　解決，解答

Develop Your Skills

〈1〉　最初から最後まで返り読みをしないで通読し，記事の内容を把握しましょう。

〈2〉　英文のチャンキングをしましょう。

〈3〉　チャンクごとに意味をとらえながら読んでみましょう。

〈4〉　チャンクごとにシャドーイングやオーバーラッピングをしましょう。

〈5〉　文章全体を理解するよう，最初から最後まで通して読んだり聞いたりする練習を繰り返しましょう。

Going Deeper

④〈those who ＋動詞〉は，「～する人々」という意味を表すフォーマルな表現です。
e.g. **Those who** would like to take this course should sign up now. このコースを受講したい人は今申し込み登録をしてください。
　また，〈those ＋形容詞（句）〉のように，who ＋ be が省略された形もあります。
e.g. **Those present** were opposed to the plans. 出席した人たちはその計画に反対した。
　The project has been a great success and I would like to thank all **those involved**. プロジェクトは大成功を収めました。私は関係者のみなさまに感謝の意を示したいです。
　文脈や場面に応じて，このようなフォーマルな表現も使えるようになりたいですね。

Summary Check

ニュースの内容に関する以下の質問に，（　　　）を埋めて答えましょう。

〈1〉　Why was the bacterium named Ideonella sakaiensis?

　　　－ Because it (　　　　) (　　　　　　　　　　　) in Sakai in Osaka Prefecture.

〈2〉　How long was the Group of 20 summit held in Osaka?

　　　－ It was held (　　　　　) (　　　　　) days.

〈3〉　How many enzymes did the bacterium use to decompose polyethylene tere-
　　　phthalate (PET)?

　　　－ It used (　　　　　) (　　　　　　　　　).

〈4〉　What surprised the global scientific community when Oda and others re-
　　　leased an article in 2016?

　　　－ It was (　　　　　) Ideonella sakaiensis feeds on (　　　　　　　)
　　　　(　　　　　　　　　).

〈5〉　What was a German team able to do in 2019?

　　　－ It succeeded (　　　　　) (　　　　　　　　　) a 3-D analysis of the other
　　　enzyme, MHETase.

Activate Your Language ② Write!

次の日本語を英語にしましょう。（太字の日本語に相当する英語は，本文で学習したものを使うこと）

〈1〉私はプレッシャー**に対処する**のがあまり得意ではありません。

　　　I'm not so good at (　　　　　　) (　　　　　) pressure.

〈2〉一部のウミガメは主にクラゲ**を常食としています**。

　　　Some sea turtles (　　　　　) mostly (　　　　) jellyfish.

〈3〉大銀行の破綻が，銀行破綻の連鎖反応**を引き起こす**かもしれません。

　　　The collapse of a major bank could (　　　　　) (　　　　　) a chain reaction
　　　of bank failures.

Activate Your Language ③ Speak!

ペアやグループで，以下の課題に取り組みましょう。

〈1〉 Let's talk!

身近な話題について，会話を楽しみましょう。

(1) How many plastic bags do you use in one week?

(2) Can you name other wild animals suffering from plastic pollution?

(3) What action do you think you can do in your daily life to reduce plastic pollution?

〈2〉 Pros and Cons

次の質問をし合ったり，Yes や No の根拠を話し合ったりしましょう。

QUESTION : Do you agree with the idea that the Japanese government should take the lead in reducing plastic waste?

－ Yes. The reasons are:

①

②

③

－ No. The reasons are:

①

②

③

第 8 章 高齢者の負担増？ 医療保険制度の今後

総語数 **408** カバー率：4000 語で **74 %** CEFR B2 で **79 %**

Activate Your Schema

　世界に類を見ない速さで進んでいる日本の少子高齢化は，国民の医療費に大きく影響しています。特に，全体の約 6 割を占める高齢者医療費の増加が，大きな社会問題となっています。高齢者医療費に占める高齢者自身の負担（保険料と税金）はごく一部で，現役世代の保険料の多くを拠出してまかなわれているのが現状です。労働人口が先細りする中，このままでは，現役世代が高齢者医療を支える構造に限界が見えます。こうした現状に，次世代の社会を担う人たちはどう対処すればよいのでしょうか。

Active Communication

　日常会話で役立つ語句や表現に親しみましょう。

A1：おじいちゃんが昨夜入院したんだ。

B1：本当？　それはお気の毒に。大丈夫？

A2：うん，ありがとう。だけどあのさ，すごく申し訳なく感じてるんだって。私たち，つまり納税者が，彼の医療費の大半を負担してるってことに。

B2：どういうこと？　もう少し詳しく教えてくれない？

A3：彼らの医療費の 90% は健康保険でまかなわれているんだよ。

B3：知らなかったな！　私たちはこの問題への意識をもっと高めるべきだね。

A1：入院する　be hospitalized
B1：お気の毒に　I'm sorry.
cf. sorry　気の毒に（残念に）思って
e.g. I feel sorry for him.　彼が気の毒だ。
A2：あのさ　You know what?
　　　納税者　taxpayer
　　　負担する　cover
　　　医療費　medical expenses

B2：どういうこと？（「どうしてそうなるの？」というニュアンス）　How come?
　　　詳しく話す　elaborate 圓
e.g. elaborate on the project
cf. elaborate the plan 囮 その計画を練る
A3：健康保険　health insurance
B3：〜を意識している
　　　be aware of 〜
　　　（賛否両論ある）問題　issue

🔊 15 **EXAMPLE**　　　　　　　　　　　※太字は特に便利な表現です。

A1: *My grandfather was hospitalized last night.*

B1: *Really? **I'm sorry to hear that**. Is he okay?*

A2: *Yeah, thanks, but you know what? He feels sorry that we, I mean, taxpayers, cover a lot of his medical expenses.*

B2: *How come? Can you elaborate on that?*

A3: *90% of his medical bills are covered by health insurance.*

B3: *I didn't know that! **We need to be more aware of this issue**.*

🔊 16 Activate Your Language ① (Read & Listen!)

Health care system could collapse if elderly people's contributions not doubled: insurance official

① Japan's universal health care system could collapse unless the medical expense burden shouldered by elderly patients aged 75 or older is at least doubled, a senior official of a nationwide health insurance group has warned.

JIJI PRESS PHOTO

② Corporate health insurance unions are facing "quite serious" financial conditions amid the country's graying population, Masahiro Sano, vice chairman of the National Federation of Health Insurance Societies, or Kenporen, said in a recent interview.

③ "There have been unions that couldn't hike premiums and had no choice but to dissolve," Sano said. Kenporen is an umbrella organization for corporate health insurance unions across the country.

④ Currently, people in the so-called late-elderly group pay 10 percent of their medical bills, with the rest covered by health insurance.

⑤ To prevent the universal health care system from collapsing, Sano said that the elderly self-coverage

---

health care system　医療制度
collapse　（建物，計画等が）つぶれる，崩壊する
contribution　寄付，貢献，保険料，拠出金，掛金
double　自 2倍になる
他 を2倍にする
① medical expense burden　医療費負担
shoulder　（責任や負担を）負う
patient　患者

② face　に面する・直面する
quite　かなり
amid　〜の中・最中に
graying　高齢化する（＝ aging）
cf. gray は「白髪の，老年の，円熟した」。頭髪がすべて白い場合 white hair，半分ほどの場合 gray hair。
vice chairman　副会長・副議長
③ hike　（家賃・物価等）を上げる（主に［米］）
premiums　保険料
have no choice but to do　（〜する）以外の方法はない
dissolve　解散する，分解する
organization　組織
④ currently　現在のところ，一般に
so-called　いわゆる
the rest　残り
⑤ prevent A from B　A が B するのを防ぐ・妨げる
e.g. Her cold may prevent her from playing in the game.　彼女の風邪は，彼女がその試合でプレーするのを妨げるかもしれない。

rate should be raised to 20 percent.

⑥ He also said there are two other options: covering elderly medical costs with taxpayer money and further increasing insurance premiums for working generations.

⑦ "The root of the problem is the (rising) cost of elderly medical expenses, but there's no prospect for its resolution," the Kenporen official said.

⑧ Since the late-elderly medical care scheme was introduced in 2008, the average annual employee income has fallen by about ¥40,000, while health insurance premiums deducted from their salaries have risen by more than ¥100,000 on average, according to Sano.

⑨ Over ¥60,000 of the premium's increase was meant for contributions to the late-elderly medical scheme, he added.

⑩ "Total contributions (to the late-elderly scheme) are expected to be more than ¥1 trillion higher in 2025 than now and this has to be shouldered by the dwindling working population," Sano said.

⑪ "The current system doesn't seem sustainable at all," Sano claimed. "I can't see any ways to avoid (an increase in late-elderly people's burden)."

⑫ Sano referred to a recent Kenporen survey showing that some elderly people are willing to accept a rise in their self-coverage rate. "Many elderly people don't want to put burdens on their children and grandchildren," he said.

⑬ In the interview, Sano also said a planned consumption tax hike from the current 8 percent to 10 percent in October 2019, chiefly designed to cover swelling social security spending, is indispensable. He even urged the government to consider a further increase.

⑥ taxpayer　納税者	
⑦ root　根，根本 prospect　見通し，見込み，予想	
⑧ deduct　を控除する on average　平均して	
⑩ be expected to ～　～すること が予想・期待されている dwindle　減少する	
⑪ sustainable　持続可能な，耐 えうる	
⑫ refer to ～　～に言及する	

⑬ hike　上昇（主に［米］）
e.g. a hike in prices　物価の上昇
swell　ふくれる，膨張する
spending　支出，出費
indispensable　不可欠な
urge　を駆り立てる，急がせる，しきりに促す
e.g. They urged him to read the book.　彼らは彼をしきりに促して その本を読ませた（彼らは彼に，その本を読むようしきりに促した）。

⑭ Kenporen, for its part, will promote efforts to help elderly people stay healthy and raise awareness among young people about medical system issues, Sano said.

⑭ promote　を促進する

[October 4, 2018　JIJI / The Japan Times]

Develop Your Skills

〈1〉　最初から最後まで返り読みをしないで通読し，記事の内容を把握しましょう。

〈2〉　英文のチャンキングをしましょう。

〈3〉　チャンクごとに意味をとらえながら読んでみましょう。

〈4〉　チャンクごとにシャドーイングやオーバーラッピングをしましょう。

〈5〉　文章全体を理解するよう，最初から最後まで通して読んだり聞いたりする練習を繰り返しましょう。

Summary Check

　ニュースの内容に関する以下の質問に，（　　　　）を埋めて答えましょう。

〈1〉　What could happen if the medical expense burden shouldered by elderly patients aged 75 or older is not at least doubled?

－ Japan's universal (　　　　　　　　) (　　　　　　　　　) system could (　　　　　　　　　).

〈2〉　What is Kenporen?

－ Kenporen is an umbrella (　　　　　　　　　　　　　) for corporate (　　　　　) (　　　　　　　　　　　) unions (　　　　　　　) the country.

〈3〉　What did Mr. Sano say is needed to prevent the universal health care system from collapsing?

－ The elderly self-coverage (　　　　　　) should be (　　　　　　　　) to 20 percent.

〈4〉 What does the recent Kenporen survey show?

    − It shows that some (   ) people are (   ) to accept a
      (   ) in their self-coverage rate.

〈5〉 According to Mr. Sano, what will Kenporen promote?

    − It will promote efforts to help elderly people (   ) healthy and
      raise (   ) among young people about medical system
      (   ).

Activate Your Language ② — Write!

次の日本語を英語にしましょう。(太字の日本語に相当する英語は，本文で学習したものを使うこと)

〈1〉今のところ，現役世代が高齢者医療費をまかなう**以外の方法はない**。

For now, working generations have (   ) (   ) (   ) to
cover elderly (   ) (   ).

〈2〉悪天候は，彼がニューヨークで開催された年次大会に出発**するのを妨げた**。

Bad weather (   ) him (   ) (   ) for
the annual conference held in NYC.

〈3〉2行目の「この全体」はどんなこと**に言及しています**か？

What does "all this" (   ) (   ) in the second line?

Activate Your Language③ Speak!

ペアやグループで，以下の課題に取り組みましょう。

〈1〉Let's talk!

身近な話題について，会話を楽しみましょう。

(1) What do we need to do to keep ourselves healthy?

(2) What should we do to help elderly people stay healthy?

(3) Do you have a chance to communicate with elderly people? If yes, how?

〈2〉Pros and Cons

次の質問をし合ったり，Yes や No の根拠を話し合ったりしましょう。

QUESTION : Do you agree with the idea of universal health care?

－ Yes. The reasons are:

①

②

③

－ No. The reasons are:

①

②

③

Going Deeper

①「肩の荷が下りる」という表現がありますが，shoulder は「肩」という名詞だけでなく，「(責任や負担を) 負う」という動詞でも使われます (**shoulder** the burden 重荷を負う)。

　こうして身体部位が動詞として使われる例に face があり，「(困難等) に直面する」という意味で頻出といえるでしょう (He **faces** a difficult situation. 彼は困難に直面している)。

　eyeball, neck, butt, elbow 等もそのまま動詞として使用されます。フォーマルな場での使用に適さないものもありますが，どのような文脈で使われるか調べてみましょう。

液体のりで幹細胞培養

総語数 **421** カバー率：4000 語で **66%** CEFR B2 で **71%**

Activate Your Schema

　白血病は，いわば「血液のがん」で，造血幹細胞（骨髄の中で血球を作り出すもとになる細胞 hematopoietic stem cells）が骨髄の中でがん化し，無制限に増殖する病気です。19 世紀後半，ドイツの病理学者ウイルヒョウ（Virchow）が発見しました。当時は治療法がなく，白血病細胞がどんどん増え続けて血液が白くなるために，白い血の病気，つまり白血病と命名されました。治療法は，抗がん剤などの化学療法や輸血などの他，骨髄移植や造血幹細胞移植治療などがあります。この造血幹細胞の培養を，市販の液体のりで大量かつ安価に行える可能性を日本人科学者が発表しました。

Active Communication

　日常会話で役立つ語句や表現に親しみましょう。

A1：有名なオリンピック水泳選手の池江璃花子さんの病気のニュースを聞いた？

B1：いや。どうしたの？

A2：彼女は白血病だと発表したんだよ。

B2：白血病？　どんな病気？

A3：簡単に言えば，血液のがん。

B3：本当？　でも，最近は新しい治療法も開発されてきているよね。

A1：水泳選手　swimmer
cf. オリンピック選手
　　Olympic athlete

A2：〜を発表する，知らせる
　　announce that 〜
　　白血病　leukemia
A3：簡単に言えば　simply put /
　　putting it simply / in short
cf. hematology　血液学
B3：治療法　treatment / cure /
　　therapeutic method

🔊 17 **EXAMPLE**　　　　　　　　※太字は特に便利な表現です。

A1: *Did you hear the news about the famous Olympic swimmer, Ikee Rikako's disease?*

B1: *No. What has happened to her?*

A2: ***She announced that*** *she has been suffering from leukemia.*

B2: *Leukemia? What kind of disease is that?*

A3: ***Simply put****, it's a hematologic cancer or a cancer of the blood.*

B3: *Really? But recently, new treatments have been developed, right?*

Activate Your Language ① Read & Listen!

🔊 18

Glue sold over counter cheapest way to cultivate stem cells

① Cheap liquid glue commonly found in stationery shops and convenience stores is a perfectly acceptable alternative to a pricey fluid normally used to culture stem cells for the treatment of leukemia patients, researchers say.

YAMATO Co., Ltd.

② Scientists from the University of Tokyo and Stanford University in the United States, published their findings in the British scientific journal *Nature* on May 30.

③ They reported being able to get mouse cells to proliferate in large numbers, which is difficult to do even with expensive solutions, using a substance from liquid adhesives found on store shelves.

④ One expert likened the development to finding "Columbus's egg," given that it could lead to a breakthrough in the way leukemia and other disorders are treated.

⑤ Hematopoietic stem cells, which turn into leukocytes and red blood cells, are difficult to proliferate even when immersed in a culturing fluid priced at tens

---

glue　接着剤，のり
cultivate　を培養する
stem cells　幹細胞

① alternative to ～　～の代替(品)
fluid　液体
culture　を培養する
patient　患者

③ proliferate　自急［激］増する，（細胞分裂等により）増殖する
solution　溶液，溶剤
substance　物質・実質
adhesive　形粘着性の　名粘着性のもの・接着剤
④ liken A to B　A を B にたとえる
given that ～　～を与えられたなら → ～と（仮定）するなら
lead to ～　～（という結果）につながる
breakthrough　飛躍的進歩
disorder　無秩序，（体等の）不調，病気
⑤ hematopoietic stem cells　造血幹細胞
leukocyte　白血球
red blood cells　赤血球
immerse　を浸す，沈める

of thousands of yen for just 500 milliliters.

⑥ For that reason, those suffering from leukemia typically seek bone marrow transplantation or receive cord blood from donors.

⑦ Satoshi Yamazaki, a specially appointed associate professor of hematology at the University of Tokyo, and his colleagues exhaustively tested components of conventional culture solutions and other substances to find a trailblazing way to proliferate the stem cells.

⑧ When they cultivated the cells in polyvinyl alcohol (PVA), the team found that the difficult-to-grow cells proliferated several hundred-fold. Transplanting the cultured cells into mice allowed the scientists to confirm that the cells can develop into leukocytes and other cells.

⑨ PVA is the major component of laundry starch and liquid glue. Yamazaki used a fluid adhesive bought at a convenience store and discovered that hematopoietic stem cells can also proliferate in the commercially available glue.

⑩ Yukio Nakamura, head of the Cell Engineering Division of the Riken research institute and a Riken BRC Cell Bank project member who co-authored the academic paper with Yamazaki and the other researchers, said he was "so astonished" that he could not believe in the finding initially.

⑪ "Every scientist would feel as if the scales fell from his or her eyes," said Nakamura, referring to the discovery.

⑫ If the new method safely allows hematopoietic stem cells to proliferate in large quantities, cell shortages associated with cord blood transplantation could be eased. It would also lessen the burden on bone marrow donors.

⑬ Yamazaki noted that other kinds of stem cell can

probably also be cultured with the technique.

⑭ "Our discovery may greatly contribute to regenerative medicine and basic research," he added.

⑮ For more information on the *Nature* article, please see (https://www.nature.com/articles/s41586-019-1244-x).

[June 10, 2019 The Asahi Shimbun]

⑭ contribute to ～　～に貢献する
regenerative medicine　再生医療
（医学）

Develop Your Skills

〈1〉 最初から最後まで返り読みをしないで通読し，記事の内容を把握しましょう。

〈2〉 英文のチャンキングをしましょう。

〈3〉 チャンクごとに意味をとらえながら読んでみましょう。

〈4〉 チャンクごとにシャドーイングやオーバーラッピングをしましょう。

〈5〉 文章全体を理解するよう，最初から最後まで通して読んだり聞いたりする練習を繰り返しましょう。

Summary Check

ニュースの内容に関する以下の質問に，（　　　）を埋めて答えましょう。

〈1〉 What was used as the alternative to the pricey fluid used to culture stem cells in the research?

－ Cheap liquid (　　　　　　　) found in stationery shops and
(　　　　　　　) stores.

〈2〉 Why aren't stem cells used so often to treat leukemia?

－ Because hematopoietic stem cells are difficult to (　　　　　　　)
(　　　　　) when immersed in pricey culturing fluid.

〈3〉 What kind of commercially available items include polyvinyl alcohol (PVA)?

    − PVA is the (   ) (   ) of
      (   ) starch and (   ) glue.

〈4〉 What was the first reaction of the researcher when finding that stem cells can
    be cultured in liquid glue?

    − He was (   ) (   ) (   ) he could not believe
      (   ) the finding initially.

〈5〉 What is the prospect of the finding?

    − This discovery may greatly (   ) (   )
      (   ) medicine and basic (   ).

Activate Your Language ②   Write!

次の日本語を英語にしましょう。(太字の日本語に相当する英語は，本文で学習したものを使うこと)

〈1〉 われわれの現在の計画**に対する**有効な**代替案**はない。

    There is no practical (   ) (   ) our current plan.

〈2〉ソーシャルメディア・サービスは，私たちが容易にコミュニケーションをとる**ことを可能にした**。

    Social media services have (   ) us (   ) communicate easily.

〈3〉喫煙は様々な国で，多くの人の死亡**に影響を与えている**。

    Smoking (   ) to many people's (   ) in various
    (   ).

Activate Your Language③ Speak!

ペアやグループで，以下の課題に取り組みましょう。

〈1〉Let's talk!

身近な話題について，会話を楽しみましょう。

（1）What kind of stationery do you often buy? What is your favorite stationery?

（2）When was the last time you went to the hospital? Why did you go there?

（3）What do you do to keep fit? What kind of activities or food do you recommend for good health?

〈2〉Pros and Cons

次の質問をし合ったり，Yes や No の根拠を話し合ったりしましょう。

QUESTION：Should organ transplants be more available in Japan?

－ Yes. The reasons are:

①

②

③

－ No. The reasons are:

①

②

③

Going Deeper

　「癌」と「がん／ガン」，つまり漢字表記と仮名表記は，厳密には違うものを指します。「癌」は上皮細胞，たとえば胃の粘膜上皮細胞の悪性腫瘍のことであり，「がん／ガン」はこれらも含め，もっと広い意味での悪性腫瘍を指します。英語では前者は carcinoma，後者は cancer です。

　「がんで死ぬ」は die of cancer / die from cancer のどちらも可能です。表現は発話者の意識や気持ちによって変化しますが，コア・ミーニングを考えるとわかりやすいです。of / from のコア・ミーニングは「の／から」でしょう。つまり，from はちょっと遠さが感じられます。The desk is made of wood. / Wine is made from grapes. は典型的な例ですが，見た目から材料がすぐにわかるなら of，そうでないなら from です。とすれば，die of / from cancer は，「がんが直接の原因で／がんの影響で（直接の死因は別で）」という意識が反映されていると考えることができます。

第**10**章　予想外？　温室効果ガスが与える食品への影響

総語数 **496**　カバー率：4000 語で **72%**　CEFR B2 で **79%**

Activate Your Schema

　近年増え続ける温室効果ガスの代表的なものは，二酸化炭素です。二酸化炭素は，主に化石燃料（石炭，石油等）を燃焼させると発生します。また，二酸化炭素を吸収して酸素を排出する熱帯雨林等の森林は，農地の拡大等のため伐採され減少しています。温室効果ガスの弊害は地球温暖化以外にも多様ですが，最も予期されなかったことの１つは，温室効果ガスが食品の栄養価を下げる可能性についてではないでしょうか。なぜそのようなことが起きるのでしょうか。そして対策はあるのでしょうか。

Active Communication

　日常会話で役立つ語句や表現に親しみましょう。

A1：地球温暖化について考えてる？

B1：考えているよ。いつも買い物に再利用が可能なエコバッグを持参しているよ。

A2：最近，温暖化が進んでいることを体感するね。

B2：うん。環境に優しい活動が，地球環境を少しずつでも改善できるといいんだけど。

A3：まず第一に，ごみの量を減らすことが必要だね。

B3：多くの人の環境意識が高くなればいいんだけど…。

A1：について考える（文脈から「意識している」という意味でとらえる）be conscious of
B1：再利用可能な reusable
A2：（温暖化が）進む→ひどくなる get worse
B2：環境に優しい environmentally friendly　少しずつ little by little
A3：まず第一に first of all　ごみの量 the amount of garbage　減らす reduce
B3：環境意識 eco-conscious

◁)) 19 **EXAMPLE**　　　※太字は特に便利な表現です。

A1: *Are you conscious of global warming?*

B1: *Yes I am. I always carry my **reusable** eco-bag with me.*

A2: *I feel global warming has been **getting worse** these days.*

B2: *Yes. I hope **environmentally friendly** activities can improve the global environment even **little by little**.*

A3: ***First of all**, reducing the amount of garbage is necessary.*

B3: *I do hope many people would be more **eco-conscious**....*

Activate Your Language① Read & Listen!

Planet-Warming Gases Make Some Food Less Nutritious, Study Says

① Rising levels of planet-warming gases may reduce key nutrient levels in food crops, according to a new study.

Voice of America

② Rice grown while exposed to carbon dioxide levels expected by the end of this century had lower levels of vitamins, minerals and protein than normal, the results showed.

③ The authors said the impact would be most significant for the poorest citizens of some of the least-developed countries, who eat the most rice and have the least diverse diets.

④ In the study, published in the journal *Science Advances*, scientists grew 18 varieties of rice in fields in China and Japan. They pumped carbon dioxide over the plants to simulate the atmosphere of the future.

⑤ Rice grown under high carbon dioxide conditions had, on average, from 13 to 30 percent lower levels of four B vitamins, 10 percent less protein, 8 percent less iron and 5 percent less zinc than conventionally grown rice.

---

planet-warming gas　温室効果ガス（greenhouse gas）

① nutrient　栄養素［物］
according to　〜によると

② expose　をさらす
cf. expose A to B　AをBにさらす
carbon dioxide　二酸化炭素

③ author　著者
impact　影響
significant　著しい
developed countries　先進国
diet　日常の（飲）食物・ダイエット
④ pump　ポンプで吸い出す，送り込む
simulate　をシミュレーションする

⑤ on average　平均して
zinc　亜鉛
conventionally　慣習的に，従来どおり

⑥ On the other hand, vitamin E levels increased by about 13 percent on average.

⑦ The results are bad news, "especially for the nutrition of the poorer population in less-developed countries, because this population depends for nutrition on rice," said study co-author Kazuhiko Kobayashi at the University of Tokyo.

⑧ That includes roughly 600 million people in Indonesia, Cambodia, Myanmar, Bangladesh, Laos and several other nations, mainly in Southeast Asia, the report said.

⑨ While research has shown higher temperatures from climate change and weather extremes will cut food production, especially in the tropics, scientists are increasingly finding that rising greenhouse gas levels are a threat to food quality as well.

⑩ Earlier studies by Harvard University researcher Sam Myers and colleagues showed that wheat, maize, rice, field peas and soybeans grown under high carbon dioxide conditions all had lower levels of protein and minerals. The scientists estimated that roughly 150 million people might be at risk of protein or zinc deficiency by 2050.

⑪ It's one example of the surprises climate change has in store, Myers said.

⑫ "If you and I sat down 15 years ago and thought about, 'I wonder how dumping enormous amounts of carbon dioxide into the atmosphere will affect our well-being,' I think one of last things we would have come up with is, 'I bet it will make our food less nutritious,' " he said.

⑬ "My concern is, there are many more surprises to come," Myers added.

⑭ He noted that global pollution, biodiversity loss, deforestation and land use change, and other human

⑥ on the other hand 一方

⑦ depend on A for B A に B を頼る
co-author 共著者

⑧ roughly おおよそ, ざっと

⑨ weather extremes 異常気象
the tropics 熱帯地方
threat 脅威

⑩ colleague 同僚
wheat 小麦
maize トウモロコシ [通例, 米・加・豪では corn]
field peas サヤエンドウ
estimate 見積もる, 推定する
at risk of 〜 〜の危険にさらされて
cf. at the risk of 〜 〜の危険を冒して
deficiency 不足, 欠乏
⑪ in store 未来・運命などが（人に）ふりかかろうとして
⑫ think about 〜を考える, 検討する
dumping A into B A を B に投棄する
affect に影響を及ぼす
well-being 健康, 幸福
bet 賭ける
e.g. I bet / I'll bet きっと
⑬ concern 懸念, 関心
⑭ global pollution 地球汚染
biodiversity loss 生物多様性の損失
deforestation 森林破壊

activities are likely to produce unexpected problems as well.

⑮ "You can't fundamentally disrupt all the natural systems that we have adapted to over millions of years of evolution without having these ripple effects that come back to affect our own health and well-being," he said.

⑯ The new study suggests a way to minimize the nutritional impact of climate change.

⑰ "Different [rice] varieties showed quite different changes in response to higher carbon dioxide concentrations," Kobayashi said. Rice breeders can use these differences to create varieties that are less affected by greenhouse gas levels, he said.

[May 23, 2018 Voice of America]

⑮ disrupt　を崩壊させる
ripple effect　波及効果 [可算名詞]
cf. ripple　さざ波, 小波

⑯ minimize ～　～を最小限に抑える

⑰ quite　かなり
in response to　～に応じて

Develop Your Skills

〈1〉　最初から最後まで返り読みをしないで通読し，記事の内容を把握しましょう。

〈2〉　英文のチャンキングをしましょう。

〈3〉　チャンクごとに意味をとらえながら読んでみましょう。

〈4〉　チャンクごとにシャドーイングやオーバーラッピングをしましょう。

〈5〉　文章全体を理解するよう，最初から最後まで通して読んだり聞いたりする練習を繰り返しましょう。

Going Deeper

みなさんは温暖化問題について何か気をつけていることはありますか？　買い物の際にエコバッグを持参するとポイントを付与するお店が増えたことで，常にエコバッグを持ち歩くという人も多いかもしれません。「環境に優しい（environmentally friendly）」という言葉もよく耳にするようになりました。近年では，複数国で展開する大企業は環境配慮の姿勢を見せるべき，との風潮があります。温暖化を改善するためには何をすればよいでしょうか？　まずはごみの分別をきちんとする，節水，節電を心がける等，各々で身近な環境に配慮する姿勢が何よりも大切かもしれません。

Summary Check

ニュースの内容に関する以下の質問に，（　　　）を埋めて答えましょう。

〈1〉 What is the reason for producing less nutritious foods?

－ It is because of (　　　　　　　　) - (　　　　　　　) (　　　　　　).

〈2〉 According to the journal *Science Advances*, where did scientists grow 18 varieties of rice to simulate the atmosphere of the future?

－ They grew them (　　　) (　　　　　　) and (　　　　　　).

〈3〉 According to Kazuhiko Kobayashi, the result of their study was bad news for less-developed countries. Why?

－ Because they (　　　　　　　) (　　　) rice (　　　) nutrition.

〈4〉 What impacts are expected if greenhouse gas levels become higher?

－ Rising greenhouse gas levels would be a (　　　　　　) to food (　　　　　　).

〈5〉 What effects are expected if farmers plant several kinds of rice together?

－ They can create varieties that are (　　　　　) (　　　　　　) by greenhouse gases.

Activate Your Language ②　Write!

次の日本語を英語にしましょう。（太字の日本語に相当する英語は，本文で学習したものを使うこと）

〈1〉長時間，肌を太陽に**さらさ**ないほうがいい。

It is better not to (　　　　　　　) your skin (　　　) the sun for long hours.

〈2〉**一方で**，環境汚染は悪化している。

(　　) (　　　) (　　　　　) (　　　　　　), global pollution is getting worse.

〈3〉最新の調査**によると**，異常気象は食料生産量を減らすようだ。

(   ) (   ) the latest survey, weather extremes will cut food production.

Activate Your Language ③

ペアやグループで，以下の課題に取り組みましょう。

〈1〉Let's talk!
身近な話題について，会話を楽しみましょう。

(1) Do you believe that eco-friendly activities are effective for decreasing CO_2? Why / Why not?

(2) How often do you buy beverages in plastic bottles?

(3) Do you pay attention to environmental problems?

〈2〉Pros and Cons
次の質問をし合ったり，Yes や No の根拠を話し合ったりしましょう。

QUESTION：Do you agree to participate in eco-friendly activities?

－ Yes. The reasons are:

①

②

③

－ No. The reasons are:

①

②

③

第11章 セラピードッグ，認知症カフェでの大きな役割

総語数 **519**　カバー率：4000 語で **73 %**　CEFR B2 で **85 %**

Activate Your Schema

「認知症カフェ」とは，自宅に引きこもりがちな認知症の高齢者や介護に悩む家族が社会参加する場として NPO 法人等が運営するカフェです。厚生労働省によれば，2017 年度の認知症カフェの数は全国で 5,863 か所に及びます。本章で取り上げるのは，セラピードッグがいる認知症カフェです。動物と触れ合うことで得られる癒し効果は広く知られ，ナイチンゲールもアニマルセラピーの利点を認めています。栃木県鹿沼市の「いぬかふぇ まいら」では，認知症の進行により表情が変わらず呼びかけにも応じなくなった女性が，セラピードッグを抱くと笑みを浮かべる等，具体的な効果も確認されています。ここでは気軽にアニマルセラピーを体験して欲しいと月 1 回のカフェを企画したり，傾聴等のボランティアを募集したりしています。

Active Communication

日常会話で役立つ語句や表現に親しみましょう。

A1：あのさあ，動物は好き？

B1：もちろんさ。実際，ラブラドールレトリバーを 1 匹飼ってるよ。

A2：へえ。その犬はかなり賢いって聞いたけど。

B2：そのとおり。将来はセラピードッグにしたいんだ。

A3：セラピードッグ？　初めて聞いたよ。

B3：病院や施設で働く犬だよ。癒しの効果があるって言われてるんだ。

A1：あのさあ，それでさあ　so
B1：もちろんさ　sure [of course / certainly / surely]
　　実際　actually
cf. 実は　in fact
A2：～って聞いたけど　I hear ～
　　かなり　quite
cf. rather / quite / fairly の順で意味が弱くなる。
B2：そのとおり　That's right.
A3：聞いたことがある
　　I have heard of ～
　　[ここでは「聞いたことがない」ので never (not) を入れる]
B3：(老人や孤児等の) 施設　home
cf. 娯楽施設 facilities for recreation，教育施設 an educational institution，軍事施設 military installations
　　～と言われている
　　It is said (that) ～
　　患者　patient

◁)) 21　**EXAMPLE**　　※太字は特に便利な表現です。

A1: *So, do you like animals?*

B1: *Sure. **Actually**, I have a Labrador retriever.*

A2: *Uh-huh. I hear that dog is **quite** smart.*

B2: *That's right. I want him to be a therapy dog in the future.*

A3: *Therapy dog? **I've never heard of that.***

B3: *They work in hospitals and homes. **It's said** they heal patients effectively.*

Activate Your Language ① Read & Listen!

((•)) 22

Therapy dogs giving comfort at dementia cafe in Tochigi

① A therapy dog cafe in Kanuma, Tochigi Prefecture, has recently begun operating as a "dementia cafe" once a month to offer an opportunity for elderly dementia patients and their families to enjoy conversation over coffee and tea.

The Yomiuri Shimbun

② Therapy dogs that comfort people are stationed at Inu Cafe Maera. The comfort brought by having contact with animals, called animal therapy, is believed to be effective for dementia patients.

③ The cafe also has staff members who have learned about dementia.

④ "With dogs, psychological barriers between people are lowered. People with dementia may be able to open up to other people and enjoy conversation," a staff member at the cafe said.

⑤ On Oct. 2 at the cafe on the outskirts of the city, a woman in her 80s put a male Labrador retriever on her lap and petted it while smiling.

---

comfort　快適さ，慰め
cf. comfortable　快適な
dementia　認知症

① prefecture　県
conversation　会話

② station　を配置する
contact with ～　～との接触，触れ合い
cf. make[lose] contact with him
彼と連絡をとる［が途切れる］

④ barrier　障害，バリア
open up to ～　～と打ち解ける
⑤ outskirts　[通例複数] 郊外，町はずれ，周辺
cf. on[in] the outskirts of ～
～の郊外・はずれに
lap　膝（座ったときに子どもや物を載せる部分）
cf. knee　膝・膝関節
pet　をなでる

⑥ A woman accompanying her said: "She hasn't developed severe symptoms yet, but we came here to prevent the progression of dementia. She is more expressive than usual."

⑦ Dementia cafes are often operated by nonprofit organizations and others to offer opportunities to participate in society for people with dementia, who tend to be reclusive, and their families, who are concerned about their care. Usually, rooms in community halls and hospitals are used for such cafes.

⑧ According to the Health, Labor and Welfare Ministry, there were 5,863 dementia cafes across the country in fiscal 2017. A Tokyo-based association promoting dementia cafes said it is unusual for a dementia cafe to have therapy dogs.

⑨ Inu Cafe Maera is operated by the Tochigi Animal Therapy Association, which trains Labrador retrievers, toy poodles and other dogs and engages in activities to allow hospital inpatients and residents at elderly facilities to have contact with these dogs.

⑩ Hoping to have more people come in contact with therapy dogs, the association opened the Maera cafe four years ago.

⑪ The cafe began the dementia cafe activity due to an experience of Tsuyoshi Hirasawa, 57, the head of the Tochigi Animal Therapy Association. On a visit to an elderly facility, he saw a resident with dementia who almost always remained silent begin to speak when touching a dog: "I had a dog long time ago, and it ..."

⑫ Surprised by the incident, Hirasawa realized how profound the impact of therapy dogs on dementia patients could be. He decided to open a dementia cafe on the first Tuesday of each month, when the cafe was usually closed.

⑬ To prepare to accept dementia patients, staff members received a lecture from a training course for de-

⑥ accompany に付き添う
severe 深刻な
symptom 症状
prevent を防ぐ・妨げる
progression 進行
expressive 表情豊かな
⑦ nonprofit 非営利の
organization 組織
participate in ～ ～に参加する
reclusive （人が）隠とん生活を好む・引きこもりがちな，（場所等が）人里離れた・隔離された
be concerned about ～ ～を懸念している，～に関心をもっている
⑧ according to ～によると
fiscal 財政上の，会計の
cf. fiscal stamp 収入印紙
Tokyo-based 東京に本社（本部）を置く，拠点とする
association 協会
promote を促進する
⑨ engage in ～ ～に携わる・従事する
allow A to do A が（～するのを）許可する，可能にする
inpatient 入院患者
cf. outpatient 外来患者
resident 居住者

⑪ remain のままである
silent 沈黙した

⑫ incident 出来事
profound 重要な
impact 影響

⑬ deal with ～ ～に対処する，～を処理する

mentia supporters held by local governments so that they can deal with such people in a proper manner.

⑭ The cafe usually offers pasta, curry and cakes. On dementia cafe days, ingredients are cooked to be tender by staff members qualified as a nursing care food specialist to enable elderly people to easily swallow them.

⑮ Other measures are also taken for elderly people, such as lightly seasoning the ingredients and removing fish bones.

⑯ "I hope ordinary people also visit the dementia cafe to make it a place where they can communicate with dementia patients and their care workers," Hirasawa said.

[October 30, 2018 The Yomiuri Shimbun / The Japan News (partially revised)]

proper　適切な
manner　方法，やり方

⑭ ingredient　材料
tender　柔らかい
qualified　資格を持った
swallow　を飲みこむ

⑮ measure　対策，処置
season　に味をつける
cf. seasoning　味つけ，調味料，薬味

⑯ communicate with 〜　〜と交流する

Develop Your Skills

〈1〉　最初から最後まで返り読みをしないで通読し，記事の内容を把握しましょう。

〈2〉　英文のチャンキングをしましょう。

〈3〉　チャンクごとに意味をとらえながら読んでみましょう。

〈4〉　チャンクごとにシャドーイングやオーバーラッピングをしましょう。

〈5〉　文章全体を理解するよう，最初から最後まで通して読んだり聞いたりする練習を繰り返しましょう。

ニュースの内容に関する以下の質問に，（　　　）を埋めて答えましょう。

〈1〉 How often does the "dementia cafe" open?

－ It opens (　　　　　) (　　　) (　　　　　　).

〈2〉 Why did the woman who hasn't developed severe dementia symptoms come to Inu Cafe Maera?

－ To (　　　　　　　) the (　　　　　　　　　　) of dementia.

〈3〉 What incident surprised Tsuyoshi Hirasawa?

－ A resident with dementia who almost always remained (　　　　　　)
began (　　　) (　　　　　　) when (　　　　　　) a dog.

〈4〉 Who cooks on dementia cafe days?

－ (　　　　　　) members (　　　　　　　　　) (　　　) a
nursing care food specialist do.

〈5〉 What measures are taken for elderly people when the cafe offers food?

－ They season the (　　　　　　　　) lightly and (　　　　　　　)
fish bones.

次の日本語を英語にしましょう。（太字の日本語に相当する英語は，本文で学習したものを使うこと）

〈1〉 その国賓が日本に滞在している間，首都には多くの警察官が**配置され**た。

Many police officers (　　　　　　　) (　　　　　　　　　) in the capital
during the state guest's stay in Japan.

〈2〉 その留学生は，クラスメート**と打ち解けて**会話を楽しむようになった。

The exchange student began to (　　　　　　) (　　　) (　　　) her
classmates and enjoy the conversation.

〈3〉彼は大学を卒業した後，金融業に**ついた[に従事した]**。

After (   ) (   ) college, he (   )

(   ) financial business.

Activate Your Language ③ Speak!

ペアやグループで，以下の課題に取り組みましょう。

〈1〉Let's talk!
身近な話題について，会話を楽しみましょう。

(1) What kind of animal do you like best? Why?

(2) Do you often go to a cafe?

(3) What do you want to do for people at elderly facilities?

〈2〉Pros and Cons
次の質問をし合ったり，Yes や No の根拠を話し合ったりしましょう。

QUESTION：Do you agree with using animals in caring for people?

－ Yes. The reasons are:

①

②

③

－ No. The reasons are:

①

②

③

Going Deeper

⑫ profound のコア・ミーニングは「深い」でしょう。この語は様々な場面で使われます。❶「(変化，影響等が) 重大な，重要な」という意味の他に，❷「(学識や考え等が) 深い，深遠な」，さらに医学的には❸「症状が重い」にもなります。コア・ミーニングがシンプルなので和訳も多様で，たとえば a profound silence は「深い静寂，まったくの無音」等と訳してもよいでしょう。文法の視点では，比較級／最上級を作る際に more / most を用いる点も興味深い，まさに profound な単語です。

第12章 ペット家電，発売増加

総語数 **561**　カバー率：4000 語で **63%**　CEFR B2 で **78%**

Activate Your Schema

　社団法人日本ペットフード協会によると，2018 年の飼育頭数は犬が約 890 万頭，猫は約 965 万頭と，猫が犬の飼育頭数を上回りました。時系列では，犬は減少傾向ですが猫は横ばいと，昨今の「猫ブーム」を反映しているようです。また同じ調査によると，ペット飼育阻害要因トップ 3 は「長期の旅行がしづらくなる」「お金がかかる」「集合住宅に住んでおりペット禁止」でした。飼育率トップを世界的に見ると，犬はブラジルの 25.0%，猫は米国の 23.0% で，日本のペット飼育率は（犬は 12.64%，猫は 9.78%）必ずしも高くないようです。さて，進化の続くペット家電，飼い主の救世主となるでしょうか。

Active Communication

　日常会話で役立つ語句や表現に親しみましょう。

A1：きみの今日の夜の予定は？

B1：まっすぐ家に帰るよ。犬のタローの散歩をさせないといけなくて。

A2：犬の散歩にどれくらい時間がかかるの？

B2：1 回 20 分ずつ。1 日 2 回散歩させるの。

A3：いい運動になりそうだね。ジムに行く必要ないね。

B3：そのとおり！　でも試験でひどく忙しいときは，犬の散歩代行の人を頼むんだよ。

A1：あなたの〜の予定は？
What is your plan for 〜？

B1：まっすぐ家に帰る
go straight home
犬を散歩させる
walk a/one's dog
〜しなければいけない
have (got) to 〜

A2：〜するのにどれくらい時間がかかるの？　How long does it take (for) you to 〜？

B2：1 日 2 回　twice a day

A3：運動　exercise
ジムに行く　go to the gym

B3：そのとおり　exactly
〜でひどく忙しい，忙殺されている
be swamped with 〜

cf. swamp 图 沼地 他 を水浸しにする，にどっと押し寄せる
犬の散歩代行者 dog-walker

◁)) 23 　**EXAMPLE**　　　　　　　　　　※太字は特に便利な表現です。

A1: *What's your plan for this evening?*

B1: *I'm going straight home. I've got to walk my dog Taro.*

A2: *How long does it take you to walk him?*

B2: *It takes me about 20 minutes each time. I walk him twice a day.*

A3: *It sounds like good exercise. You don't have to go to the gym.*

B3: *Exactly! But when I'm swamped with exams, I hire a dog-walker.*

Activate Your Language ①

More home appliances for pets hitting store shelves

① An increasing number of home appliances for pets are hitting the shelves, such as cameras that allow owners to watch the adorable actions of their dogs and cats from outside their home.

② Home appliance makers are beefing up efforts to develop high-quality products, pinning their hopes on an increasing trend of pet owners who are willing to spend more money, as they regard pets as family members.

③ A 54-year-old company employee and his wife in Higashiosaka, Osaka Prefecture, both work, so their toy poodle is left at home during the day on weekdays. The man said he is worried about their pet during the working day. "The dog is a part of our family. I wished there was a camera that allowed me to watch it during my spare time at work," he said.

④ Reflecting the sentiments of such pet owners, Panasonic Corp. will release a camera in December that takes images of pets at home and other places and sends live video to the smartphones of far-away owners. A sensor of the camera detects the pet, enabling the lens to track it, even if they run around. The camera will also be equipped with a function to record video footage.

⑤ Sharp Corp. will also release an air purifier that has a special mode for dogs and cats on Nov. 15. If owners register a dog or cat, the air purifier will release a breeze for dogs, which are normally more sensitive to the heat, and refrain from releasing wind flow to cats, which are more sensitive to the cold.

---

home appliance　家庭電化製品
hit (the) store shelves / hit the shelves　（商品が）店頭に並ぶ，発売される
① an increasing number of ～　～が増えている（コア・ミーニングは「～の増加中の数字」）
allow A to do　A が（～するのを）許可する，可能にする
adorable　かわいい，愛らしい
② beef up　強化する，増強する
pin hopes on ～　～に期待をかける
cf. pin　をピン留めする，（希望等）をかける
regard A as B　A を B とみなす，考える
③ prefecture　県（ここでは「府」）
on weekdays　平日に，平日には
cf. on weekends　週末に
spare time　空き時間

④ sentiment　気持ち，心情
release　を発売する
live video　生中継動画
far-away　遠く離れた
detect　を検知する，見つける
enable A to B　A が B するのを可能にする
track　を追跡する
be equipped with ～　～を備えている・装備している
video footage　ビデオ映像
⑤ air purifier　空気清浄機
register　を登録する
breeze　微風，そよ風
be sensitive to ～　～に敏感である，～に弱い
refrain from ～ ing　～を控える，やめる

⑥ Sharp entered the pet-related home appliances market in July with a cat toilet that automatically records data on cats such as the cat's weight and the frequency and amount of urination. Owners can also apply for a paid service that notifies them of abnormalities of cats that are detected in changes of recorded data. "We aim to post sales worth ¥10 billion [$89.37 million] in the pet appliance field within two years," an official in charge of the appliances said.

⑦ An analyst who specializes in the home appliances market said the 2011 Great East Japan Earthquake, which affected numerous pets as well as people, has become a turning point that made the public realize anew the strength of the bond between owners and their pets. This became a catalyst for home appliance makers to step up efforts to develop products for pets, the analyst said.

⑧ According to the Tokyo-based Japan Pet Food Association, about 18.44 million cats and dogs were pets in 2017, exceeding the human population of those aged under 15, which was about 15 million.

⑨ As the number of owners who keep their pets indoors as family members increases, the monthly average spending for pets hit ¥18,293 ($163) — combining the figures for dogs and cats — increasing by about 45 percent in five years.

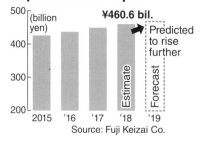

Market for pet-related products in Japan

¥460.6 bil.

500
(billion yen)
400
300
200

Estimate

Forecast

Predicted to rise further

2015 '16 '17 '18 '19

Source: Fuji Keizai Co.

The Yomiuri Shimbun

⑥ frequency 頻度，回数
urination 排尿
apply for 〜 〜を申請する・申し込む
notify A of B A に B を知らせる
abnormality 異常，異常な状態
cf. abnormal ⇔ normal
aim ねらう，目指す (to, at, for)
post sales 売上を計上する
cf. post を郵送する，簿記の元帳に記載する

⑦ the Great East Japan Earthquake 東日本大震災
affect に影響を及ぼす
turning point 転機，岐路
anew 改めて，再び，もう一度
catalyst 触媒（の働きをする人［もの］），きっかけ
step up を強化する，さらに力を入れる

⑧ according to 〜によると
Tokyo-based 東京に本社（本部）を置く，拠点とする
association 協会
exceed を超える，上回る

⑨ spending 支出，出費
hit 〜に達する，〜に至る
figure 数字，合計，総額
combine を結びつける，合わせる

⑩ Market research company Fuji Keizai Co. estimates the market size of pet-related products will be ¥460.6 billion ($4.11 billion) in 2018, a 2.4 percent rise from the previous year.

⑪ "There is an increasing trend of spending more money on pets against a backdrop of a decrease in the number of children and a tendency to marry later," said a director of Dentsu Inc. who conducts research on pet-related home appliances. "I expect the number of companies that enter the pet business market will continue to increase."

[October 27, 2018 The Yomiuri Shimbun / The Japan News]

⑩ market research　市場調査・分析
estimate　見積もる，推定する
billion　10 億

⑪ against a backdrop of 〜　〜を背景にして
cf. backdrop　（劇場の）背景幕，背景
decrease　減少
cf. increase　増加
conduct research on 〜　〜についての研究を行う

Develop Your Skills

〈1〉　最初から最後まで返り読みをしないで通読し，記事の内容を把握しましょう。

〈2〉　英文のチャンキングをしましょう。

〈3〉　チャンクごとに意味をとらえながら読んでみましょう。

〈4〉　チャンクごとにシャドーイングやオーバーラッピングをしましょう。

〈5〉　文章全体を理解するよう，最初から最後まで通して読んだり聞いたりする練習を繰り返しましょう。

ニュースの内容に関する以下の質問に，（　　　）を埋めて答えましょう。

〈1〉　What will Panasonic Corp. release in December?

　　　 − It will release a (　　　　　　　) that takes images of (　　　　　) and sends
　　　 (　　　　) (　　　　　　　) to the smartphones of far-away owners.

〈2〉　What will the camera also be equipped with?

　　　 − It will also be (　　　　　　　) (　　　　　) a function to (　　　　　　)
　　　 video footage.

〈3〉　What will Sharp Corp. release on November 15th?

　　　 − It will release an (　　　　　) (　　　　　　　　) that has a special
　　　 (　　　　　) for dogs and cats.

〈4〉　What has become the turning point that made the public realize anew the
　　　 strength of the bond between owners and their pets?

　　　 − It was the (　　　　　) (　　　　) (　　　　　) (　　　　　　　　　).

〈5〉　Why is there an increasing trend of spending more money on pets?

　　　 − It is because of a (　　　　　　　) in the number of (　　　　　　　)
　　　 and a tendency to (　　　　　) later.

次の日本語を英語にしましょう。（太字の日本語に相当する英語は，本文で学習したものを使うこと）

〈1〉「ルンバ」のようなお掃除ロボットは**家電製品**の中で人気がある。

　　 Robotic vacuum cleaners such as "Rumba" are popular among (　　　　　　)
　　 (　　　　　　　　　).

〈2〉その会社は，忙しいペットの飼い主のための革新的な**商品を開発する努力を強化している。**

　　 The company is (　　　　　　　) (　　　　) (　　　　　　　) to (　　　　　　)
　　 an innovative (　　　　　　　) for busy pet owners.

〈3〉私は気温の変化に**弱い** [**敏感である**]。

I am (　　　　　　　　　　) (　　　) changes in temperature.

Activate Your Language ③ · Speak!

ペアやグループで，以下の課題に取り組みましょう。

〈1〉Let's talk!
身近な話題について，会話を楽しみましょう。

(1) What is your favorite home appliance? Why?

(2) What new home appliance would you like to buy if you get some money?

(3) What kind of new home appliances do you think will be invented in 10 years?

〈2〉Pros and Cons
次の質問をし合ったり，Yes や No の根拠を話し合ったりしましょう。

QUESTION：Recently, many companies have developed robotic pets. Do you think it is a good idea to buy one?

‒ Yes. The reasons are:

①

②

③

‒ No. The reasons are:

①

②

③

Going Deeper

　製品の開発から店頭販売までに関連する英語表現を見てみましょう。

　新製品を開発し (develop a new product)，それを発売する (release[launch] a new product) と，店頭に並びます (hit the shelves)。それと並行して，宣伝をします (advertise)。認知度を高め (raise its awareness)，売上を伸ばす (boost its sales) ためですね。売上が10億円に達し (hit 1 billion yen)，売れ筋商品 (bestselling product) として稼ぎ頭 (cash cow) になるのが製品開発者の夢ですが，果たして現実は…。

第 13 章　アニメの逆輸入

総語数 **568**　カバー率：4000 語で **64%**　CEFR B2 で **75%**

Activate Your Schema

　ジャポニスムを知っていますか？　フランス語 Japonisme（英語では Japonism）で，19世紀にヨーロッパで流行した日本趣味のことです。19 世紀中頃の万国博覧会（国際博覧会）への出品等をきっかけに，日本美術（浮世絵，工芸品等）が注目され，西洋の作家たちに大きな影響を与えました。たとえば，リビエールは葛飾北斎の技法を取り入れ，ルイ・ヴィトンは家紋をヒントにロゴを作ったと言われています。1876 年には "japonisme" という語がフランスの辞書に登場しました。近年，日本のアニメや漫画が輸出され世界的に注目されつつありますが，フランスではその傾向が特に強いようです。そして今回の話題は，なんと「アニメの逆輸入」です。

Active Communication

　日常会話で役立つ語句や表現に親しみましょう。

A1：どんなアニメが好き？

B1：魔法や超能力を使うアニメ。君は？

A2：日常的な学園生活を描いたものかな。

B2：ああ，生徒が弁当を食べるシーンが世界に影響を与えたらしいよ。

A3：どういうこと？

B3：ヨーロッパの人たちが，弁当箱の中にフルコース料理が入っていると驚いたって。

A1：どんなアニメが〜ですか？
What（kind of）anime 〜?

B1：超能力　supernatural power
君は？［「あなたはどうですか？」という意味で］
How about you?

B2：弁当を食べる
eat[have] a (box) lunch
（bento が使われることもある）
に影響を及ぼす　affect

A3：*cf.* 言葉の（真の）意味等を尋ねる場合は by を使う。
e.g. What do you mean by "No"?
No とはどういう意味ですか？

◀)) 25　**EXAMPLE**　　　　　　　　※太字は特に便利な表現です。

A1: *What kind of anime do you like?*

B1: *I like anime where people use magic or supernatural powers.* ***How about you?***

A2: *Anime of everyday life in school.*

B2: *Oh, I've heard that a scene of students eating bento lunches has affected the world.*

A3: ***What do you mean?***

B3: *European people were surprised to see that a bento box has a full course meal in it.*

26

Activate Your Language ① | Read & Listen!

DISCOVER ANIME / Reverse phenomenon of 'Radiant'

① While new anime series "Radiant" might look like a conventional animation filled with fantasy and adventures, it is actually an epoch-making piece of pop culture developed through exchanges between France and Japan.

©2018 Tony Valente, ANKAMA EDITIONS / NHK, NEP

② Currently being broadcast on NHK-E, the anime features Seth, a misfit trying to become a "great wizard," who lives in a world where "Nemesis" creatures descend from the sky to attack people. The creatures can also give people supernatural powers enabling them to become wizards.

③ NHK Enterprises producer Yusuke Fujita first learned about "Radiant" when he stumbled across the first volume of the manga, published by Asuka Shinsha, in a bookstore in 2015.

④ "Where has this been hiding?!"

⑤ For a person who thought they were up-to-date with current trends, the discovery surprised him. The fact that it was a translation of a comic by a French mangaka, 34-year-old Tony Valente, was also a shock.

---

phenomenon　現象，事象
圏 phenomena

① conventional　慣習的な，従来の
fantasy　空想・幻想
actually　実際
epoch-making　画期的な

② currently　現在のところ，一般に
NHK-E　NHK E テレ
feature　〜を呼びものにする・特集する　图 特徴
misfit　環境にうまく順応できない人
wizard　魔法使い
descend　下る，おりる
enable A to B　A が B するのを可能にする
③ stumble　つまずく・よろめく，偶然出会う
e.g. stumble on[over] a stone 石につまずく / stumble on[across] a typographic error　偶然誤字を見つける
⑤ up-to-date　最新の，現代的な
cf. out-of-date　旧式の，時代遅れの

⑥ Fujita, 31, read the manga and was immediately absorbed.

⑦ "I couldn't believe a French person created it. It was a quintessential shonen boys' manga," he recalled.

⑧ A big fan of "Dragon Ball," and "One Piece," Fujita always dreamed of working on a mainstream fantasy series for NHK. He was well aware of the frequent fierce battles to obtain visualization rights in the anime industry, but as "Radiant" was not widely known at the time, he was confident he could get them.

⑨ Fujita secured the rights to produce an anime adaptation after contacting the publisher in France when the fourth volume of the manga came out in 2016. He commissioned animation studio Lerche, which was responsible for "Ansatsu Kyoshitsu" (Assassination Classroom) among others, to produce the series.

⑩ NHK's executive producer Yuko Yonemura is another person who was captivated by the story.

⑪ "Not only is the work exciting, but it also includes important issues such as immigration and discrimination," said Yonemura. "I'm positive it fits the principles of the programs we broadcast for children in the early evenings on Saturday on NHK-E," she said.

⑫ This is the first time a French manga has been turned into an anime in Japan.

⑬ Japanese anime started being aired widely in France in the late 1970s and almost developed into a social problem because of how absorbed in them children became. Many manga titles were translated into French in the 1990s. The children who grew up in those days are the ones who are now in the center of the latest "Japonisme" cultural exchange.

⑭ While France has its original version of highly ar-

---

⑥ absorb を吸収する・夢中にさせる

⑦ quintessential 典型的な (typical)

⑧ mainstream 主流の
be aware of 〜 〜に気づいている・知っている
fierce どうもうな，激しい
obtain を獲得する

⑨ secure を安全にする，確保・獲得する
adaptation 適応，改造・脚色
commission A to do A に〜するよう委任・依頼・命令する

⑩ captivate を魅了する・うっとりさせる

⑪ not only A but (also) B A だけでなく B も
immigration （入国する）移住・移民
cf. emigration（出国する）移住・移民 [→ p.93 Going Deeper]
discrimination 差別

⑬ the latest 最近の，最新の
Japonisme フランス語でジャポニスム。英語では Japonism。
⑭ bande dessinée バンド・デシネ（ベルギー・フランス等を中心とした地域の漫画）
a number of 〜 かなりの〜，いくつかの〜（前者が一般的。数量をわかりやすくするため a large[great/small] number of 等のように用いることもある）

tistic bande dessinée comics, a considerable number of artists now draw Japanese-style manga.

⑮ "The numbers are quickly increasing," said Masato Hara, 44, who translated "Radiant" into Japanese. "And they're popular."

⑯ The publication of "Radiant" in Japan is a reverse phenomenon in terms of manga being exported. It's understandable such news is being enthusiastically discussed in France.

⑰ "It still feels like a dream to me," said Valente on Sept. 14, after attending a preview at NHK Broadcasting Center in Tokyo.

⑱ Valente talked about his own experience of facing discrimination in France because his father wasn't originally from the country. "I suppose you can see such encounters reflected in my work," he said.

⑲ Manga is no longer a field confined to Japan — nor are there boundaries to the attraction it is generating. And that is exactly what the release of "Radiant" demonstrates.

⑳ "Radiant" is broadcast from 5:35 p.m. on Saturdays on NHK-E.

[October 27, 2018 The Japan News]

⑯ publication　出版（物）・発行・発表

⑰ still　今なお

⑱ face　に面する・直面する
encounter　（偶然の）出会い，遭遇
⑲ no longer　もはや～ない
nor　［否定の節・文の後に用いて］
…もまた～ない（倒置文となる）
e.g. She didn't go, nor did her friend.　彼女は行かなかった，また彼女の友人もそうだった。
confine A to B　A を B に限る，制限する
boundary　境界（線），限界
attraction　魅力
generate　～を引き起こす，生じさせる
that is exactly what ～
（what の後に文が続き）それがまさに～するものだ

Develop Your Skills

〈1〉 最初から最後まで返り読みをしないで通読し，ニュースの内容を把握しましょう。

〈2〉 英文のチャンキングをしましょう。

〈3〉 チャンクごとに意味をとらえながら読んでみましょう。

〈4〉 チャンクごとにシャドーイングやオーバーラッピングをしましょう。

〈5〉 文章全体を理解するよう，最初から最後まで通して読んだり聞いたりする練習を繰り返しましょう。

Summary Check

ニュースの内容に関する以下の質問に，（　　　）を埋めて答えましょう。

〈1〉 How did the NHK producer Mr. Fujita know of "Radiant?"

　　－ He (　　　　　　　　) (　　　　　　　　　　) the manga in a bookstore.

〈2〉 Why did Mr. Fujita think he could get the visualization rights of "Radiant" easily?

　　－ Because "Radiant" (　　　　　) not widely (　　　　　) at that time.

〈3〉 Why was Ms. Yonemura captivated by the "Radiant" story?

　　－ Because the story is (　　　　　) (　　　　　　) exciting (　　　　) it also includes important social issues.

〈4〉 How many French people draw Japanese-style manga now?

　　－ A (　　　　　　　　) number (　　　) artists do it.

〈5〉 What did the release of "Radiant" demonstrate?

　　－ Manga is (　　　) (　　　　　　) a field confined to Japan.

Activate Your Language ② 〔Write!〕

次の日本語を英語にしましょう。（太字の日本語に相当する英語は，本文で学習したものを使うこと）

〈1〉 我々の工場の改修によって，より多くの自動車を生産**することが可能になるだろう**。

　　The renovation of our factory will (　　　　　　) us (　　　) produce more automobiles.

〈2〉 この論文は，英語の学習者が**直面している**問題のいくつかを示している。

　　This paper (　　　　　　　) some of the problems (　　　　　) by learners of English.

〈3〉「それが，**まさに**私の言いたいことなのだ！」と彼は喜んで答えた。

　　"That's (　　　　　　) (　　　　　　　) I want to say!", he responded with joy.

Activate Your Language ③ Speak!

ペアやグループで，以下の課題に取り組みましょう。

〈1〉 Let's talk!
身近な話題について，会話を楽しみましょう。

(1) How long do you watch TV for every day?

(2) What do you know about France?

(3) What anime do you like?

〈2〉 Pros and Cons
次の質問をし合ったり，Yes や No の根拠を話し合ったりしましょう。

QUESTION : Does anime have bad effects on young people?

－ Yes. The reasons are:

①

②

③

－ No. The reasons are:

①

②

③

Going Deeper

　フランスでは日本のアニメや漫画が人気です。カンヌ国際映画祭からアニメーション部門を独立させて創設された，アヌシー国際アニメーション映画祭や，日本の現代および伝統文化を幅広く紹介する Japan Expo（ジャパン・エキスポ）が毎年開催されています。

② wizard（魔法使い・魔術師）は民話・幻想文学・アニメ・漫画にしばしば登場します。他には witch, sorcerer, mage, magician 等と呼ばれます。

⑪ Not only A but (also) B は重要な構文です。「A だけでなく B も」という意味ですが，A と B で重きが置かれるのは B です。類似の表現に B as well as A があります。重要な B を最初に言い，その後に「A と同様に」と付け加える表現です。つまり，類似の表現であっても A と B の順番が逆になります。

⑭ bande dessinée（バンド・デシネ）は，ベルギー・フランス等の地域での漫画です。略称は B.D.（ベデ）で，バンデシネとも呼ばれます。「描かれた帯」というフランス語に基づいており，意味は「続き漫画」，英語では comic strips に相当します。

第 14 章 多文化共生，日本を 我が家と呼ぶアメリカ人

総語数 **570**　カバー率：4000 語で **78%**　CEFR B2 で **83%**

Activate Your Schema

　日本に住む外国人がますます増えています。外国語教育の充実と地域の国際交流推進を目的とした JET プログラム（The Japan Exchange and Teaching Programme）では，語学指導を行う外国青年招致を行い，地方自治体等で任用しています。台湾に生まれアメリカで育った 1 人の女性が，このプログラムの ALT（アシスタント語学教師）として日本の三重県四日市市に赴任し，この場所を「自分の家」と呼ぶようになりました。国籍や文化が異なる者同士がうまくやっていくにはどうすればよいのか，この例を通して考えてみましょう。

Active Communication

　日常会話で役立つ語句や表現に親しみましょう。

A1：どのくらい日本に住んでいるの？　10 年くらい？

B1：これまで 8 年間住んでいるよ。その前は最も人口の多い国，中国に住んでいたよ。

A2：ああ，そうなの。ところで，日本では 1 人暮らし，それとも誰かと一緒に住んでいるの？

B2：ホストファミリーの家にいるよ。彼らとの生活は毎日楽しいよ。

A3：彼らとけんかすることはないの？

B3：ないね。実際のところ，この家族の一員のように感じているよ。

A1：10 年　a decade
cf. 20 年　two decades

B1：人口の多い　populous

A2：ところで　by the way
1 人で　alone

B2：ホストファミリーと住む
stay with my host family

A3：けんかをする
have an argument

B3：のように感じている
feel like ～
実際　actually

🔊)) 27　**EXAMPLE**　　　　　　　　※太字は特に便利な表現です。

A1: *How long have you been in Japan? About **a decade**?*

B1: *I've lived here for 8 years. But I lived in the most **populous country**, China, before I came here.*

A2: *Oh, I see. By the way, do you live alone or with someone?*

B2: *I stay with my host family. I enjoy my life with them every day.*

A3: *Don't you **have any arguments** with them?*

B3: *No. Actually, I **feel like** I am a part of the family.*

Activate Your Language ① Read & Listen!

28

JET Programme Voices / Multicultural symbiosis

symbiosis　共存，共同生活

① My name is Wan Jung (Amy) Lin. I was born and raised in Taiwan, and I immigrated to the United States in 2005. I came to Japan as an Assistant Language Teacher on the JET Programme and was placed in Yokkaichi City, Mie Prefecture, in July 2013. I have been living there for the past five years and just finished my time on the JET Programme in July 2018.

① immigrate　移住する
place　を置く，配置する
cf. placement　置くこと，配置，配属
prefecture　県

Wan Jung (Amy) Lin / Special to The Japan News

② I still remember when I was informed of my placement by email from the JET Programme office back home. When notified I would be going to Mie Prefecture, I had many questions. Where is Mie? What is Yokkaichi, a market? (The city's name can be read that way.) Yokkaichi is known for Yokkaichi asthma? Why did JET do this to me? Will I die there?

② still　今なお
asthma　喘息

③ Of course I didn't. Instead, I fell in love.

③ fall in love　恋に落ちる
cf. I fell in love with her.　彼女に恋をした。

④ Yokkaichi is the most populous city in Mie Prefecture. Its location is perfect: convenient for shopping, hiking, rock climbing, or relaxing by the beach. I fell in love with the Suzuka mountain range right away

④ populous　人口の多い

and expanded my horizons to hike in many prefectures with many Japanese friends.

⑤ Soon after my arrival, I joined several local groups. I only learned the hiragana writing system before coming to Japan, so I had to do my self-introduction in the simplest Japanese. I was caught off-guard when asked for a detailed self-introduction.

⑥ I found myself in this situation repeatedly, so my Japanese friends and colleagues helped. They would typically tell people my name, and immediately explain that I was Taiwanese but moved to America at a young age, and I do in fact speak English fluently.

⑦ It was difficult for some people to accept not only that America is my country of citizenship but that I am in fact an American. After all these years of acculturation in California, it was hard when people tried to tell me otherwise.

⑧ However, I eventually found my comrades. I was transferred to a local junior high school where roughly 30 percent of the students have roots in other countries. Not until then did I know that Mie Prefecture has one of the biggest JSL (Japanese as a second language) populations in K-12 education in Japan. Even many in Mie are unaware of this fact.

⑨ I felt at home at this school. Many of the students are called by one name at school, and another name at home. They speak one language at school, and another at home. This is common in California, but not too many Japanese friends had experience with this dynamic.

⑩ I shared my identity crisis with my students, and many of them understood. In this school, it is everyone's responsibility to support their friends and classmates. The entire school curriculum is focused on diversity and JSL. The students are proud to be part of such a diverse community. Even for me, the ALT, this was important.

⑤ local　地元の
self-introduction　自己紹介
off-guard　油断して，警戒を怠って
be［get］caught off-guard
不意［隙］を突かれる，油断に付け込まれる
⑥ colleague　（主に職業上の）同僚
cf. coworker　同僚，（一緒に仕事をする）協力者
typically　典型的に，例によって，決まって
fluently　流暢に
⑦ not only A but (also) B　A だけでなく B も
country of citizenship　国籍
cf. citizenship　市民権，公民権
acculturation　（子どもの成長期における）文化的適応，（異文化の接触により生じる）文化変容
⑧ eventually　ついに
comrades　同志，仲間
transfer　を移す，転任させる
roots　［複数形で］(人の) ルーツ (人の民族的，文化的，社会的な起源)
cf. root　根，根本
Not until then did I ～　その時になって初めて私は～［倒置による強調］
K-12　幼稚園から高校卒業までの教育
be unaware of ～　～を認識していない
cf. be aware of ～　～を認識している
⑨ dynamic　動力，動き

⑩ be focused on ～　～に焦点が置かれて
diversity　多様性
be proud to be ～　～であるのを誇りに思う

⑪ Of course, throughout this time I made and kept many close friendships with Japanese people. This five-year experience was a reconciliation journey for me. I took things for granted when I was in California, but my friends here in Yokkaichi helped me to reexamine who I really am.

⑫ My definition of being Taiwanese-American has evolved, and I know that will continue. The same goes for my students and neighbors in Mie. I call this city home because it is where I grew as an international person.

[October 30, 2018 The Japan News (partially revised)]

⑪ reconciliation　和解，一致，調和
take ～ for granted　～を当然ととらえる
reexamine　を再吟味（試験，検査）する

⑫ definition　定義
evolve　進化する，展開する
The same goes for ～　それと同じことが～にも当てはまる

Develop Your Skills

〈1〉　最初から最後まで返り読みをしないで通読し，記事の内容を把握しましょう。

〈2〉　英文のチャンキングをしましょう。

〈3〉　チャンクごとに意味をとらえながら読んでみましょう。

〈4〉　チャンクごとにシャドーイングやオーバーラッピングをしましょう。

〈5〉　文章全体を理解するよう，最初から最後まで通して読んだり聞いたりする練習を繰り返しましょう。

Summary Check

ニュースの内容に関する以下の質問に，（　　　　）を埋めて答えましょう。

〈1〉　What is Wan Jung Lin's ethnicity?

－ She was (　　　　　　) and (　　　　　　　　) in (　　　　　　　　　　) but immigrated to the U.S.

〈2〉　How long has Wan Jung Lin lived in Yokkaichi City?

－ She has lived (　　　　　　　　) (　　　　　　) (　　　　　　　) years.

〈3〉 What did Wan Jung Lin learn before she came to Japan?

 – She learned (   ) (   ) write hiragana before coming to Japan.

〈4〉 What was the feature of the junior high school to which Wan Jung Lin transferred?

 – Roughly 30 percent of the students (   ) their ( ) ( ) other countries.

〈5〉 Why does Wan Jung Lin call Yokkaichi home?

 – Because it is (   ) she grew as ( ) (   ) person.

Activate Your Language ②   Write!

次の日本語を英語にしましょう。(太字の日本語に相当する英語は, 本文で学習したものを使うこと)

〈1〉中国は約15億人いる最も**人口が多い**国である。

 China is the most (   ) country (   ) about 1.5 billion people.

〈2〉彼は車**だけでなく**バイク**も**持っている。

 He has ( ) (   ) a car (   ) a motorcycle.

〈3〉あなたの幸せの**定義**は何ですか？

 What is your (   ) of happiness?

Activate Your Language ③

ペアやグループで，以下の課題に取り組みましょう。

〈1〉 Let's talk!

身近な話題について，会話を楽しみましょう。

（1）Which country would you like to visit? Why?

（2）Have you met people from overseas in Japan? When and where?

（3）What do you think about your cultural identity?

〈2〉 Pros and Cons

次の質問をし合ったり，Yes や No の根拠を話し合ったりしましょう。

QUESTION : Do you want to be an exchange student?

− Yes. The reasons are:

①

②

③

− No. The reasons are:

①

②

③

Going Deeper

　辞書では immigrate は「移住する」と表記されていますが，emigrate にも同じく「移住する」とあります。このように，形が似ている語は意味も似ている場合が多くありますが，それぞれニュアンスは異なります。immigrate の意味は主に「（人が外国から）移住してくる」，emigrate の意味は主に「（人が外国へ）移住する」です。つまり「入ってくる」と「出ていく」の違いがあり，これはそれぞれの語の冒頭 im- / e- からも感じ取れますね。import（輸入する）と export（輸出する）の関係に似ています。また，migrate という語もあります。意味は「（人や動物が）一地方から他地方へ移住する，移動する」で，動物も含めて「移動する」という意味合いです。ニュースではよく「難民」も話題になりますが，英語では refugee です。難民は単なる「移動，移住」ではなく，政治，宗教，戦争等の危機的状況のためやむを得ず国外へ逃れます。和訳では「避難者，亡命者，逃亡者」等になることもあります。このように類似語との違いも意識しておくと，インプットでの理解が深まるだけでなく，アウトプットでも適切に使用できます。

Important Sentences 重要センテンス一覧

第1章————————
The airline company **is expected to** start its test flights in early November.

その航空会社は，テスト飛行を11月初旬に始める**と予想されている**。

It's **a big step toward** realizing delivery services using cutting-edge technologies.

それは，最新技術を利用している配達サービスを実現すること**への大きな一歩**だ。

Packages of documents **weighing up to 2 kilograms** will be transported to their destinations **in about 10 minutes.**

2kg までの重さの書類の小包は，**約10分で**目的地に運ばれるだろう。

The group **aims to put the service into commercial use** mainly in remote areas.

そのグループは，主にへき地で**そのサービスを商用利用することを目指している**。

第2章————————
The new market **consists of** several sophisticated buildings.

その新しい市場は，いくつかの洗練された建**物から成り立っている**。

Some **feel relieved that** the glass walls separate the sales floors from visitors.

そのガラス張りの壁が売り場フロアを観光客から切り離している**ことに安心している**人もいる。

The public **is allowed to** enter the wholesale market on weekdays.

一般の人々は，平日に卸売市場へ入場すること**が許可されている**。

Many tourists stand in front of the truck and pose **for their friends to take a photo** of them.

多くの観光客はそのトラックの前に立ち，ポーズをとって，**友達に写真を撮ってもらう**。

第3章————————
The number of international students has **more than doubled**, with 424 enrolled in fiscal 2017 compared with 178 in fiscal 2010.

留学生の人数は，2017年度に424名が入学しており，2010年度の178名に比べて**2倍よりも多くなった**。

Foreign enrollment has **more than tripled** to 240 in the seven years through fiscal 2017.

外国人入学者数は，2017年度までの7年間で**3倍を超え**，240人となった。

Trainees from China **accounted for** 31.6 percent of the total in fiscal 2017.

中国からの研修生は，2017年度には全体の31.6%**を占めた**。

The Japanese food industry has high hopes the trend will **help boost sales** of Japanese food around the world.

日本の食品業界は，その傾向が世界における日本食の**売上を増やすのに貢献する**ということに，高い期待を持っている。

第4章————————————————

The government **concluded an agreement on** technical cooperation.

政府は，技術協力に関して**協定を締結した**（合意の結論に達した）。

The capacity of the water tank is 200L.

水タンク**の容量は** 200 リットルである。

A mist generator will **be added to** the Flower Merry-Go-Round.

ミスト発生装置はフラワーメリーゴーランド**に追加される**だろう。

People can stay in public spaces **with comfort** in summer.

人々が公共の場所で夏を**快適に**過ごすことができる。

第5章————————————————

Japanese people are **more conscious about** their looks **than** people overseas.

日本人は容姿に関して海外の人々**よりも意識している**。

The percentage was **higher than we had expected**.

その割合は，**われわれが予想していたよりも高かった**。

The survey was conducted **in response to** calls for an overview of the market.

その調査は，その市場の全体像を求める声に**応じて**実施された。

Problems **associated with** medical cosmetic treatments are commonly reported in Japan.

美容医療施術**に関連した**問題は，日本ではよく報告されている。

第6章————————————————

Amid an increase in the number of Muslims, exchange activities are expanding.

イスラム教徒の数が増加する**中で**，交流活動は広がっている。

He recognized that he did not know much about Islam **despite the fact that** Muslims had protected the Buddhist statues.

イスラム教徒がその仏像を保護してきた**という事実にもかかわらず**，彼は，自分がイスラム教について多くを知らないと認識した。

Local people **viewed** the meeting with Muslims **as** a rare opportunity.

地元の人たちは，イスラム教徒との会合を珍しい機会**とみなした**。

A series of learning sessions can **lead to** mutual understanding.

一連の勉強会は相互理解**につながる**ことがある。

第7章

Methods for dealing with the contamination of marine environments by plastics are expected to be a major theme of the conference.

プラスチックによる**海洋環境汚染に対処する方法は**，その会議の主要テーマになる**見通し**だ。

She was **among those who** were part of a team that discovered the bacterium.

彼女は，そのバクテリアを発見したチームに属している**人々の中に**いた。

PET **was long believed not to be biodegradable**, as it is produced **using petroleum**.

PET は**長い間生物分解できないと信じられていた**，それが**石油を使って**生成されるので。

A British team **succeeded in improving** the ability of the enzyme to decompose plastic.

ある英国のチームは，プラスチックを分解する酵素の能力を**改善することに成功した**。

第8章

To **prevent** the health care system **from** collapsing, the self-coverage rate for elderly people should be raised to 20 percent.

医療制度が崩壊する**のを防ぐ**には，高齢者の自己負担率が 20% に引き上げられるべきである。

Corporate health insurance unions are **facing serious financial conditions**.

企業の健康保険組合は，**深刻な財政状況に直面している**。

The root of the problem is the cost of medical expenses for elderly people, but **there's no prospect for** resolving this.

その問題の根本的原因は高齢者の医療費であるが，これを解決すること**への見込みはない**。

I **can't see any ways to** avoid increasing the medical expense burden of elderly people.

高齢者の医療費負担増を回避するための**いかなる方法も**，私には**見つからない**。

第9章

There is no practical **alternative to** our current plan.

われわれの現在の計画**の**，有効な**代替案**はない。

This finding will **allow** scientists **to** create new treatments for the disease.

この発見は，科学者たち**が**その病気の新しい治療法を生み出す**ことを可能にする**だろう。

He was **so** astonished **that** he could not believe in the results initially.

彼は**とても**驚いた**ので**，最初はその結果を信じることができなかった。

This research will **contribute to** the development of new medicine.

その研究は，新薬の開発**に貢献する**だろう。

第10章────────────

Rising levels of planet-warming gases **may reduce** key nutrient levels in food crops.

温室効果ガスが上昇する度合いは，作物の主要栄養素の値（栄養価）**を減少させるかも**しれない。

On the other hand, vitamin E levels **increased by about 13 percent on average**.

一方，ビタミンEの値は**平均して約13%増加**した。

The scientist **estimated** that roughly 150 million people might be **at risk of** protein or zinc deficiency by 2050.

その科学者は，2050年までにはざっと1億5,000万人がタンパク質もしくは亜鉛不足**の危機にさらされ**るかもしれないと**推計し**た。

Global pollution, deforestation, and other human activities are likely to produce unexpected problems.

地球汚染，森林破壊，その他の人間の活動は，予想外の問題を生み出す可能性が高い。

第11章────────────

Animal therapy **is believed to** be effective for dementia patients.

アニマルセラピーは，認知症患者に効果的で**あると信じられている。**

With dogs, **psychological barriers between people** are lowered.

犬がいることで，**人と人との心理的なバリアー**は低くなる。

She is **more expressive than usual**.

彼女は**いつもより表情豊か**だ。

He realized **how profound** the **impact** of therapy dogs **on** dementia patients could be.

セラピードッグの認知症患者**への影響**がどれ**ほど深く**なり得るかに，彼は気がついた。

第12章────────────

An increasing number of home appliances for pets are **hitting the shelves**.

ますます多くのペット用の家電製品**が発売されている（店頭に並んでいる）。**

This became a catalyst for home appliance makers to **step up efforts to** develop products for pets.

これ（震災）が，家電メーカーがペット用品**を開発する努力を強化する**きっかけとなった。

About 18.44 million cats and dogs were pets in 2017, **exceeding** the human population of those aged under 15.

2017 年には，約 1,844 万匹のネコとイヌがペットとして飼われており，これは 15 歳未満の人口を**上回っている**。

As the number of owners who keep their pets indoors as family members increases, the monthly average spending for pets **hit** ¥18,293 ($163).

家族の一員としてペットを室内で飼う人の数が増えるにしたがい，ペットに対する毎月の平均支出は 18,293 円（163 ドル）に**達した**。

第 13 章──────────

The creatures can give people supernatural powers **enabling** them **to** become wizards.

その生物は，人々**が**魔法使いになる**のを可能にする**超能力を，彼らに与えることができる。

Not only is the work exciting, **but** it **also** includes important issues such as immigration and discrimination.

わくわくさせる**だけでなく**，その作品は移民や差別といった重要な問題を含んで**もいる**。

This is the first time a French manga has been turned into an anime in Japan.

フランスの漫画が日本でアニメになったのは，**これが初めてである**。

He talked about his own **experience of facing** discrimination in France.

彼は，フランスで差別に**直面した**彼自身の**経験**について話した。

第 14 章──────────

Soon after my arrival in Mie prefecture, I joined several local groups.

三重県に**到着した後すぐ**，私はいくつかの地元の集まりに加わった。

Not until then did I know that Mie Prefecture is a beautiful place.

そのときになって初めて，私は三重県が美しい場所であること**を知った**。

Throughtout this time I made and kept many close friendships with Japanese people.

この時間を通して，私は日本人とたくさんの親密な友情を築き，そして保った。

My definition of being Taiwanese-American has evolved, and I know that will continue.

台湾系アメリカ人であることの私の定義が進化してきた，そしてそれが続くとわかっている。

MEMO

MEMO

各章の執筆担当は次のとおりです。桝原（1，9，13），佐藤（2，6），畠山（3，12），恒安（4），南部（5，8），吉原（7），有江（10，14），和久（11）。Goodier は全体にわたる助言・確認を行いました。

編 著

日本メディア英語学会　英語教育・メディア研究分科会

監修・執筆

桝原 克巳（ますはら かつみ）　日白大学

執 筆

有江 和美（ありえ かずみ）　　武蔵野大学

佐藤 文子（さとう ふみこ）　　中央大学

恒安 眞佐（つねやす まさ）　　芝浦工業大学

南部 匡彦（なんぶ ただひこ）　国際短期大学

畠山由香子（はたけやま ゆかこ）　お茶の水女子大学

吉原 学（よしはら まなぶ）　　東京経済大学

和久 健司（わく けんじ）　　　帝京平成大学

Jason Goodier（ジェイソン・グディアー）　帝京平成大学

執筆協力

大坪 久子（おおつぼ ひさこ）　　岡﨑 伸一（おかざき しんいち）

北村 友宏（きたむら ともひろ）　中村 俊佑（なかむら しゅんすけ）

野口 知美（のぐち ともみ）

ニュース英語で4技能を鍛える
インプットからアウトプットへ

2020 年 3 月 30 日　第 1 版発行

編 著——日本メディア英語学会
　　　　英語教育・メディア研究分科会

発行者——前田俊秀

発行所——株式会社　三修社
　　　　　〒 150-0001
　　　　　東京都渋谷区神宮前 2-2-22
　　　　　TEL 03-3405-4511 / FAX 03-3405-4522
　　　　　振替 00190-9-72758
　　　　　https://www.sanshusha.co.jp
　　　　　編集担当　松居奈都

印刷所——壮光舎印刷株式会社

© The Japan Association for Media English Studies
(JAMES) English Education and Media Research SIG
2020 Printed in Japan
ISBN978-4-384-33495-1 C1082

装幀 —— 土橋公政
準拠音声制作 —— 高速録音株式会社

教科書準拠 CD 発売
本書の準拠 CD をご希望の方は弊社までお問い合わせください。